CREOLE BOY

An autobiography of a young multiracial Black kid growing up in New Orleans, Louisiana, during the '60s and '70s.

By Herman J. Galatas Sr.

Halo
PUBLISHING
INTERNATIONAL

Halo Publishing International
8000 W Interstate 10, #600
San Antonio, Texas 78230

First Edition, April 2023
ISBN: 978-1-63765-205-3
Library of Congress Control Number: 2022904333

Halo Publishing International is a self-publishing company that publishes adult fiction and non-fiction, children's literature, self-help, spiritual, and faith-based books. We continually strive to help authors reach their publishing goals and provide many different services that help them do so. We do not publish books that are deemed to be politically, religiously, or socially disrespectful, or books that are sexually provocative, including erotica. Halo reserves the right to refuse publication of any manuscript if it is deemed not to be in line with our principles. Do you have a book idea you would like us to consider publishing? Please visit www.halopublishing.com for more information.

To my wife: You endured through some difficult days. May God bless you because of the exceptionally large cross you have had to carry.

To my late sister: With one verbal statement—*"I'm tired of Black men like you always making excuses not to go back to college and finish your degree"*—you changed my arrogance and provoked me to finish my college degree at the age of thirty-five.

Thank you, Dianne, for waking me up!!!!!

To my two adult children: For their encouragement. You were annoyed, bored, and tired of hearing these stories repeatedly, especially during Sunday-afternoon dinner. One day, you guys shouted, "DAD, WE DON'T WANT TO HEAR ANOTHER STORY. PLEASE, PLEASE STOP. WRITE A BOOK!!!!"

Great idea, Herman and Naomi, THANKS!!!!!!

To my mom: You carried me for nine months and beyond.

"And ye shall know the truth, and the truth shall make you free."

—John 8:32 (King James Version)

"Surely goodness and mercy shall follow me all the days of my life:

And I will dwell in the house of the LORD forever."

—Psalms 23:6 (King James Version)

My two angels—Goodness and Mercy—have followed me all my life. There will be several events in this book that will positively attest to the fact that they were there protecting me. Because, without them, there would not be a book.

Thank you, GOD!!!

Contents

Chapter III   70

The Awakening

Racism, Society, and God

Chapter IV   94

Back to Creole Village

My Favorite Quote

*"Yeah, I have a couple of them [problems].
I was born Black, and I was born poor."*

*—Detective John Shaft's response when
asked,"You got problems, baby?"
Shaft, 1971 classic movie*

Introduction

There is a Bible scripture that is often quoted and quoted incorrectly. "Ye shall know the truth, and the truth shall "set you free." That is not the correct wording of John 8:32 in the King James version. Correctly stated, it is "ye shall know the truth, and the truth shall make you free." "Make," not "set" you free.

To be "set free" is to release a person, animal, or object that is bound by or to something. To "make" is to create something; it involves the process of producing, creating, and educating or developing an object in order to achieve the desired outcome.

Many people find themselves in later stages of their lives still going through life's trials and misfortunes. They cannot understand why they are experiencing recurring, prolonged difficulties. They are in denial regarding many of their lives' real past circumstances. If they do not face those realities and life truths, they find themselves living as exiled characters. They have not been able to comprehend their full potential. They still have questions about their future and their potential of the future because they cannot face the truth about their past, socially, economically, or spiritually, whether good or bad. Therefore, they are still trying to find the present-day truth about their existence.

Our true-life experiences have made us who we are, good or bad. We should never deny those true experiences because it is from those substances of life that we have been "made" and why we are who we are. At later stages of our lives, we evolve, improve, and adapt, and modify behavior through education, knowledge, and adult experiences.

Therefore, I can now translate John 8:32 in this way, "You shall know the truth, and the truth shall make you understand who you are." If during the "making" there have been some misfortunes, we should accept the reality of those misfortunes and try not to repeat them. We learned from all situations in the past, whether good or bad, and we should try not repeat immoral deeds, circumstances, or mishaps because understanding the true history of our life experiences should teach us what to do and what not to do. Facing and accepting the true making of how our past behaviors/characters have been developed, allows one to modify what need to be altered so we can then be "set free" to correct what wrongs have occurred.

So now, in this book, I give you the
"true making" of Creole Boy.

I was born March 15, 1958, and I loved my experiences growing up. Yes, my exceptionally light skin complexion and my light-brown, curly hair are what I was born with. Imagine that. Mulatto was a racial description used in the 1800s and early 1900s; it categorized a race of people who were born of White and Black parents. Had I been born one hundred years earlier, I would have been classified as Mulatto, but the majority of light-complexion Black people in New Orleans today and when I was growing up describe themselves as Creole.

Pictures of me: three years old in the photo booth at Woolworth's on Canal Street; five years old in kindergarten at Saint Philip the Apostle school; and ten years old, fourth grade, Epiphany Catholic School.

Creole can best be defined today as a state of mind and of heritage.

Being Catholic...send one's children to a parochial school.

It means membership in one of the social clubs like the Autocrat or the Original Illinois.

Attention paid to observing birthdays, Baptisms, and First Communions.

Cooking a great gumbo, buying groceries (going to the supermarket) or going to the Quarter (visiting the French Quarter), and referring to two o'clock in the afternoon as evening.

Presenting one's teenage daughter to society at a debutante party. (Mary Gehman, *The Free People of Color of New Orleans*)

As the New Orleans population grew during the late 1800s and early 1900s, there were two Mulatto/Creole neighborhoods in proximity to the French Quarter. On the north side of the French Quarter, one of those areas was called Tremé. On the east side of the French Quarter, the other area was called Faubourg Marigny. My parents, grandparents, great grand-parents, and great/great/grandparents were born and raised in these two areas. The people who lived in these two areas contributed their skills and labor to the building and eco-nomic growth of New Orleans during the late 1800s and early 1900s. People who lived in these two communities often walked to work in the French Quarter, the Central Business District, and Riverfront. The Tremé and Faubourg Marigny areas are referred to as downtown, while the Anglo-Saxon/Irish/Italian/Jewish/German communities to the west and northwest side of the French Quarter are referred to as uptown.

How did this Mulatto/Creole culture come about? His-tory tells us that along with French citizens who migrated to Louisiana from Canada during the 1700s, France banished the neglected and outlaws of France to New Orleans. Men and women, but mostly men, of European descent were sent to New Orleans to serve prison terms and/or work for their freedom.

> To establish a population in the new settlement, France sent prisoners, slaves, and bonded servants...France then sent "wives" for the colonists: about ninety women from Paris jails, a wild group chaperoned by Ursuline nuns until they were married. Later, poor girls of good reputation were also recruited to bring the settlement a core of respectability, but by then the ribald side of New Orleans's lifestyle had been established. (www.city-data.com/us-cities/The-South/New-Orleans-History)

Because of the demand for free labor throughout the South, slavery was sanctioned. The French Quarter needed women for cooking, doing laundry, cleaning homes, and providing child care. Because New Orleans was really just considered the "quarters of the French"—and had no fields to plant, no fields to plow, no cotton to pick, no sugar cane to cut down—the majority of female slaves or "free women of color" worked in the French Quarter's homes and businesses, performing all of the domestic chores. Many of these ladies lived in small buildings—called "slave or servant quarters"—in the back of the locations where they worked.

What takes place when you have men together with women, no matter from what culture? White Frenchmen had relations with women of all races, with whomever was available: African slaves, free women of color, or Native American women. Therefore, the children born out of these interracial affairs were often of fair skin complexions. The regularity and frequency of these interracial affairs created a race of light-complected people of color who became known as Mulattoes or Creoles. They were of Black heritage, but their skin complexions and facial features did not resemble those descended from one-hundred-percent-native Africans. In due course, Mulatto/Creole people procreated with other Mulattoes/Creoles; consequently, a race of light-complexion Mulatto/Creole people started to populate New Orleans.

Not having many affordable places to live in the French Quarter and along Esplanade Avenue, housing developments expanded beyond the French Quarter. The traditional "shotgun" houses and many other types of homes started to develop in neighboring areas—along the north side of the French Quarter, Tremé; to the east, Faubourg Marigny. These two areas were known for housing many Mulattoes/Creoles and free people of color.

If a reader of this book does not believe this is how the New Orleans Mulatto/Creole community evolved, then research the history of New Orleans *plaçages* and *quadroons* and read the *New York Times* best seller, *One Drop* by Bliss Broyard. When tracing her family roots back to New Orleans, Ms. Broyard did research and gave a phenomenal account of free people of color in New Orleans and of the Creole culture.

The purpose of this introduction was not to do an entire historical documentation or research account of the Mulatto/Creole culture in New Orleans, which Ms. Broyard and numerous other writers have already done, but rather to document my personal Creole/Mulatto lineage and heritage. While conducting my research, some of the material I used came from www.usgwarchives.net/la, www.usgwarchives.net/la/orleans/birth-alpha, the 1900, 1920 USA census, and *Polk's New Orleans City Directory 1850 through 1948.* Here is what I discovered in my family's heritage.

My Grandmother Valetta Levy's Lineage

I am a person of mixed heritage—Black/White/French/German/Irish. One of my mother's grandfathers on her mom's side was John Levy, my great-grandfather. He was married to my great-grandmother, Alma "Wilson" Levy. According to the 1920 USA census, they lived at 1860 Burgundy Street, Faubourg Marigny neighborhood, two blocks from the French Quarter.

Their race was listed as Black (B-Color) on the census report, and they were the parents of my maternal grandmother, "Maletta," which actually should have been Valetta, Levy. John Levy's job, based on the 1920 census, is listed as a "laborer in the cotton warehouse." He was a "wage" earner according to that census. He probably helped stockpile the cotton products and inventoried cotton, possibly at the old cotton warehouses in the Marigny area.

During my research, I could not find any additional information on John Levy or Alma Wilson prior to 1920 as a family, but I did find that John Levy, as a young man, from 1888 through 1892, lived at 76 Marigny Street; in 1911, he lived at 1221 Saint Claude Avenue and was listed as a carpenter in Polk's directory.

After John Levy died, in 1933, my great-grandmother Alma Levy lived at 1230 Touro Street when my grandmother Valetta was thirteen years old. In 1945 or 1946, Alma Levy lived at 1809 Dauphine Street, in the rear location of that house (the old slave/servants' quarters), one block from the French Quarter. In the early fifties, Alma Levy moved into a small detached building, which had also been an old slave/servants' quarters, behind the house of her daughter, my aunt Thelma Levy Lockett Spencer, at 2320 Pauger Street. Alma Levy lived there until her death.

My Grandfather Sidney Moore's Lineage

My mother's great-great-grandfather on her dad's side was Louis Evalture Charbonnet, and in 1851 he lived on the corner of Barracks and Conde (now Charters Street) in the French Quarter. He and Alice Benoit, "a native of Germany" who lived at 46 Elmira Street in New Orleans (Algiers Point), had a daughter, Regina Ann Charbonnet, who was born on September 5, 1872, and is my mom's grandmother. On Regina's birth certificate, she is described as a "French child," meaning she did not resemble a person of African/Black American heritage. Regina would eventually become the mother of my maternal grandfather, Sidney Moore Jr. In 1877, Louis Evalture Charbonnet (widowed by that time) lived at 305 Charters Street in the French Quarter; there is no mention of his occupation.

My mother's great-grandfather was Ernest Joseph Moore, and he was married to Angelle Fernand; they lived at 448 Marais Street in 1880. In the State of Louisiana birth files, there is a "White" female born on April, 27, 1865, with the last name Fernand, no first name, and she was born to Rossman Fernand and Adele Morgan. If this is Angelle, then she was born White, and she would have been fifteen years old when she and Ernest birthed Sidney Joseph Moore Sr. on July 12, 1880.

Sidney Joseph Moore Sr. married Regina Ann Charbonnet on December 9, 1908. This was the union of two Mulattoes. In the 1920 census, Sidney Joseph Moore Sr. and Regina Ann lived at 1814 Saint Claude Avenue, and their races were listed as ML—Mulatto; his occupation was recorded as "presser" at 1835 Burgundy Street.

Sidney Joseph Moore Sr. and Regina Ann, in 1928, were said to live at 1910 Pauger Street, and he was recorded as owner of a "cleaners" at that location. Their younger son Sidney Jr. was born while they lived there. Young Sidney Jr. worked in the family business as a tailor. Sidney Sr. and Regina Ann later moved to 2021-½ Rocheblave Street, their final move.

One personal observation regarding Regina's age—her age on the 1920 USA census report is thirty-six. If so, then her birth year would have been 1884. I have a copy of her birth certificate, which confirms she was born in 1872. So my only conclusion about this age discrepancy is that she probably did not want people to know she was twelve years older than Sidney Sr., who, as I have already stated, was born in 1880.

As a kid, I remember my great-grandmother Regina and that long, beautiful hair. My mom would take my sister and me to visit her on Rocheblave Street during the early sixties. She was indeed a "French child," as stated so elegantly on her birth certificate. Her complexion was noticeably light. I am sure people thought her race was White back in the sixties and before.

She lived in a very large fourplex home that my grandfather, Sidney Jr. (her son), owned. She lived downstairs on the right side, while Sidney Jr. lived on the left, next to her. Regina's home was always immaculate when we visited her, not a spot of dust anywhere.

My grandfather, Sidney Joseph Moore Jr., my mom's dad, married Valetta Levy, and in 1939/40 they lived at 1814 North Villere Street, which is where they were when my mother was born on December 31, 1939. My mom tells stories about how they had chickens in the backyard, and she would chase them. In 1944/45, Sidney Jr. was listed in the census as a "laborer"; he and Valetta resided at 1422 Annette Street. Sidney and Valetta would later divorce while my mother was a teenager. Valetta then remarried my step-grandfather, Gilbert Pratts, my hero.

My Dad, Herman M. Wynne's Lineage

My dad was Herman M. Wynne, born in 1903, and his dad was Joseph Vincent Wynne, born in 1857 to Bob Wynne and Alimie, or Alinie, Wynne. I cannot find any additional information on Bob and Alimie before 1857. According to *Polk's New Orleans City Directory, 1850 through 1948*, in 1885, Joseph V. Wynne was listed as living at #7 Saint Ann Street in the French Quarter, and from 1889 to 1893, he is listed as living at 166 Spain Street; in 1894, he lived at 145 Urquhart Street. His family probably lived with him at those locations because my dad had brothers and sisters born in 1887, 1889, 1891, and 1893, as shown on the 1900 census.

When Joseph filed the 1900 USA census report, he and his wife Alina's address was 1738 Spain Street, and their family race is recorded "B," Black. I can conclude, without Joseph V. Wynne's birth certificate, that he was a multiracial person and had to be of a fair complexion to live in that area of town in 1900.

What is interesting is that after Joseph died in 1911, my grandmother, Alina Edmond Wynne, filed the 1920 census card for the Wynne family as head of household, and she recorded the family race as "MU," Mulatto. Their address in 1920 was 1605/1607 Mandeville Street. My dad was seventeen years old when his mother documented their family race as "MU," or Mulatto. Alina had to be Mulatto or White. I came to that conclusion because she took the initiative of filling out the census report of 1920. Knowing she had been married to a multiracial person too, she decided to classify her family accordingly.

Years later in 1928, my dad at twenty-five years old was probably living on his own, or with one of his brothers, because his address as head of home during my research was shown at 119 Marigny Street, and he worked in a paper factory, where he lost a couple of fingers.

My perseverance in researching my family was to provide fact-based birth dates, race, and living locations, and to establish the facts that my present-day family's roots go back over 150 years. We are profoundly and truly New Orleanians, direct descendants from the French Quarter, Tremé and the Faubourg Marigny areas, where free people of color, Blacks, Creoles, and Mulattoes lived.

I can thoroughly conclude that I am not just African American or Black. Senseless federal and state laws of the early 1900s, written and motivated by discrimination, declared that if a person had one percent of Black or African blood, then they were to be labeled as Black only. Unconscious, self-doubting politicians of authority created laws regarding people's legacies. Duh, what do you do with the other ninety-nine percent? Ninety-nine percent is a "passing grade" of A at any level of education.

Mom, Sister, and me, Easter Sunday, 1969, my grandparents' front yard.

My mother was and still is an exceptionally beautiful Creole Black woman. As a small child, when accompanying my mother in public, I would get terribly upset and wanted to fight older men when I knew they were flirting with her. My maternal grandmother was one of the most beautiful women in New Orleans during the early 1900s, according to my stepgrandfather Gilbert. My mother and grandmother were extremely attractive women, and men—Black or White—would take notice.

My sister, Dianne, was three years older than I am. My sister's father was not of Creole/Mulatto descent; therefore, my sister and I had different physical features. But it never bothered us.

My dad was a very fair, light -complected Creole/Mulatto. If you looked at him, you could tell he had a lot of "cream in his coffee." Just looking at him, a person's initial assessment of my dad at first site would not conclude he was of African/Black American heritage. My research and census information from the early 1900s show that my dad lived in several areas of the city where Blacks probably did not live at the time, and he owned several businesses in other Creole areas where Blacks scarcely owned businesses. Therefore, as a result, I concluded that perhaps, for a period, my dad "passed" for White. Later on, I found hard evidence to support that.

Picture of my dad, Herman M. Wynne, better known as Slim, possibly in the early fifties.

During the forties, fifties, and beyond, "Mulatto" was no longer used to describe race in the New Orleans metro area, nor was it used in the census as a race classification for people born from interracial unions or people of multiracial lineage. People of color were to be classified only as Colored first, then Negro, and eventually Black. Thoughtless One-Drop law!

Chapter I

Creole Village

The Beginning

I was born in 1958, at New Orleans's Charity Hospital, like most Black people in New Orleans during that period. During the fifties, if you were Black, you were probably born either in Charity Hospital or at home.

> *Physicians who have trained at Charity often refer to it as "Mother Charity, the great stone womb" that gives birth to multiple offspring and becomes "the great stone breast" that nurtures them all their lives. Charity has endured even the most difficult times. It was unquestionably needed in a city like New Orleans, which throughout its history has adopted a liberal policy towards the poor, while itself enduring much poverty. (John Salvaggio, New Orleans' Charity Hospital)*

Charity Hospital, Tulane Avenue, Downtown New Orleans, Louisiana.

Growing up in what I called Creole Village was one of the best experiences any person could have. My description of Creole Village may be different from that of other New Orleanians. To me, it was an area starting at Florida and Elysian Fields Avenues, then south on Elysian Fields Avenue to Saint Claude Avenue and North Rampart Street, then west on North Rampart Street, to Saint Peters Street and Basin Streets and Orleans Avenue where the Municipal Auditorium intersects, then north on Basin Street and Orleans Avenue to Broad Street, then east on Broad Street to Florida Avenue, then back to Elysian Fields.

The area north of Florida Avenue, on the north side of the canal, was referred to as Sugar Hill, and there were numerous Creole people of a very fair complexion that lived in that area; they probably attended Saint Leo the Great Church. I did not include this area in my Creole Village description because I hardly ventured into that area and did not know any families or have any friends from that area during my childhood. Years later, one of my mom's friends moved her family to that area.

In my Creole Village, some of the churches, schools, and businesses were:

- Saint Augustine Church on Tremé Street and Governor Nicholls Street
- Corpus Christi Catholic Church and School on Saint Bernard Avenue and North Galvez Street
- Epiphany Catholic Church and School on Duels Street and Saint Anthony Street
- Saint Augustine Catholic High School on London Avenue (renamed A. P. Tureaud Avenue)

- The Circle Theater on the corner of Saint Bernard Avenue and North Galvez Street

- The Circle Food Store on the corner of Saint Bernard Avenue and North Claiborne Avenue

- Joseph S. Clark High School on North Derbigny Street and Bayou Road

- The Chez Helene Restaurant-Bar on the corner of North Robertson and Laharpe Streets

- Lavata's Seafood-Oyster Bar on North Claiborne Avenue behind the Circle Food Store

- Jones Elementary Public School on Annette Street

- The Autocrat Club for Men on Saint Bernard Avenue

- Eddie's Restaurant and Bar on Law Street

- Mule's Restaurant on the corner of North Laharpe and North Derbigny Streets

- Cohn's Clothing Store on the corner of Annette Street and North Miro Street

- Two Brothers Bar on the corner of Saint Anthony Street and North Roman Street

- Dooky Chase Restaurant on Orleans Avenue and North Miro Street

- Triangle Lawnmowers and Bike Shop on Saint Bernard Avenue

- Rhodes Funeral Home on North Claiborne Avenue

- COUP (Community Organization Urban Politics) on North Galvez Street and London Avenue

- The Social Aid and Pleasure Club for Men on North Miro Street

- Harden Playground bound by Law Street, Allen Street, New Orleans Street and North Dorgenois Street
- Millers Grocery Store on the corner of Annette Street and North Tonti Street

There were many other businesses, mom-and-pop grocery stores, bars, barbershops etc., too many to mention. Sorry if I left your favorite location out of the list.

O'Reilly Street

The first place or location my mom said we lived was a small apartment above a little corner bar on Saint Bernard Avenue and North Miro Street. I was an infant at the time; therefore, I can't remember that experience.

The first place I remember living was a shotgun double on O'Reilly Street, between New Orleans Street and Allen Street, in the heart of Creole Village. I was either two or three years old.

Second home we lived in on O'Reilly Street in the Seventh Ward.

One of only two memories I have of that area of Creole Village was watching airplanes flying overhead in the sky while my sister and I played outside one day. The other memory includes a Creole family who lived across the street. They were very nice neighbors, and occasionally they would babysit my sister and me. On one occasion, we were in their home, watching on TV a dance show that was produced locally by the CBS affiliate, channel 4WWL. The dance show was called the *John Pela Show*. The babysitters, being teenagers or young adults at the time, were dancing along with the music on the TV. That's all I remember of O'Reilly Street.

Pauger Street

We moved from that shotgun double on O'Reilly Street to an apartment complex on Pauger Street, at the corner of Villere Street. This genuinely nice two-bedroom apartment we lived in was located on the end corner of the building, up on the second level. I can remember standing with the front door to the apartment wide open, looking south towards the CBD (central business district). I was amazed at the height of the buildings in downtown, when really they were not that tall at all in the early sixties.

This fourplex building on Pauger Street, New Orleans,
is identical to the build we lived in.

One Shell Square, the Plaza Tower, and the Marriott Hotel, which are three of the tallest buildings in New Orleans today, had not yet been built, but the buildings that were there back in the early sixties were tall enough for a three- or four-year-old boy to gaze at every day in wonder while living in Creole Village.

Living in that apartment taught me one thing. Never try to sneak a soft drink (soda) out of the tall refrigerator, especially if you are only two feet tall and the refrigerator is seven to eight feet tall.

One midday while an early toddler and home with my mom, she insisted that I, first, finish eating my lunch before I could have a soft drink, which is what we called a soda. If I did not eat all my lunch, I would not get any soft drink. Soft drink were a major treat for little kids back in the sixties, and to drink some along with your meal or after your meal was literally a reward. So, I started to eat my lunch, and my mom went into another room in the apartment to get something. As soon as she did, I disobeyed my mom and stopped eating my food. I wanted that drink desperately, and I was determined to get that drink without my mother's permission.

I started on my mission of disobedience and opened the large refrigerator door. The shelving was remarkably high, and the large glass bottle happened to be on the top shelf. I tried to reach up high to get it, but I could not reach it while standing on the floor. Therefore, I decided to step up onto the bottom floor of the refrigerator while reaching for the bottle on the top shelf. Still, I could not reach it, so I started to get up on my tiptoes to reach it. I finally was able to just touch the bottle with my hand. Back then, soft drinks were in thick glass bottles, and some of those bottles were large. Simultaneously, as I further strained on tiptoes to extend my reach so that I could grab hold of the bottle, my feet slipped, and I lost my balance. Trying to catch myself, I lost the grip I had on the bottle, and I fell backwards onto the floor now lying on my back.

That large glass bottle tumbled off the top shelf and fell right on my face, four or five feet down. It hit me in the mouth and knocked out my two front teeth. You can see my toothless grin in the first-grade picture I've included in this book. I started screaming, crying, and blood was everywhere.

My mom raced into the room frantically, not knowing what happened. She looked at me, looked at the refrigerator door wide open, and looked at the bottle on the floor. No!! She did not spank me. I was in enough pain already, so she cleaned up everything. Her only comment, *"I think ya learned ya lesson; don't do dat again."*

I was an instantaneous snaggletoothed kid for the longest. That bottle knocked out those two front teeth just as a shotgun shoots holes in a wall. Several weeks later, my mom gave me a four-year-old birthday party, and there I was, at my party with no front teeth. It seemed to take a hundred years before those two teeth ever grew back.

Across the street from the apartment was a corner grocery store, and when we would visit to shop for groceries, I remember the men in the store would ask me to smile. I would, and they would giggle and laugh and call me "snag-a-puss." It was all in good fun. They would then give me a piece of candy as a "lagniappe," and I loved that.

Aunt Thelma—Grandma Alma

The apartment we lived in on Pauger Street in Creole Village was right up the street from my great-aunt Thelma Lockett and great-grandmother Alma Levy, who also lived with Aunt Thelma in a back apartment, or servants' quarters. Aunt Thelma was my mom's aunt, and Alma was my great-grandmother. Grandma Alma and John Levy were the parents of two girls, my great-aunt Thelma and my grandmother Valletta; they also had two boys, my great-uncle Herman and my favorite uncle Jimmy.

Many people in New Orleans call their aunts Aint-Tee—for example, Aint-Tee Debra or Aint-Tee Bernice. Just part of the culture. My aunt Thelma's first name began with a *T*; therefore, I think that is why we called her Aint Tee—not Aint-Tee Thelma, just Aint Tee.

Aint Tee was of dark complexion, heavyset, beautiful lady with a lovely and wonderful laugh. When she laughed, it was delightful to hear. In the Seventh Ward's Creole Village, she was the queen of hair pressing and dressing, the process which involved Black female patrons getting their hair straightened with a hot comb. She owned her home and her business, a beauty salon; she owned real estate too. Yes, a Black woman in the fifties and early sixties in New Orleans owned a home, a business, and real estate that included rental apartments behind her home in Creole Village.

Aunt Thelma Levy Lockett Spencer,
businesswoman/neighborhood leader/trailblazer.

Aint Tee's beauty salon was very professionally designed for that era. It was a genuine, unique beauty salon built in the front part of her house; it had all the trimmings of a real beauty salon. There was a huge advertisement sign that hung outside above the steps, in the front of the home, with a spotlight that would light it up at night. During the summertime, we would sit outside on the porch at night, under that light.

Courtesy was the standard of the day, so as people walked by while we sat on the porch at night, everyone would speak. The most common response was "good night" or "good evening." Most of them knew Aint Tee, so they would say, *"Good night, Ms. Lockett,"* and her response would be *"Good night to y'all too."*

Aint Tee had to be the best hair presser (hot-comb person) in the area. The reason I say this is because older ladies and young girls would line up every day, waiting to get their hair washed and/or straightened—every day, except Sunday and Monday.

My aunt's beauty salon was a very specialized place to press hair. There were two hot-comb stations. The salon chairs were bolted to the floor, and there was a small shelf affixed to the wall behind each chair. Right above the shelf coming out of the wall was a copper-pipe extension, through which natural gas flowed. That copper pipe was screwed on to what I can only describe as these small hot-comb burners. Those were little square, gas-fired ranges that stood on four small legs, and the fire in them constantly burned at a low level. The comb burners were designed to hold the metal hot-pressing combs.

Aint Tee would place the pressing combs on the comb burners. As ladies would sit in both chairs, Aint Tee would move from one chair to the other, stroking the hot comb through the hair of one lady, until the comb became cold; then she would put that cold comb back on the burner and move over to the next chair and repeat the process. Also in this room was a hair-washing station in the back corner, where a big concrete sink was built into the wall. There was a chair in front of the sink and a drainboard that came up the back of the chair, where the ladies would place their necks to get their hair washed.

There was also an area in the beauty parlor that had two more chairs bolted to the floor; they were hair-drying stations. After the ladies would get their hair washed, they had to get it rolled, and then under the hair dryers they went. Now, these hair dryers were not just your everyday hair dryers; these things were humongous. When a lady would sit under one, it was as if she were a space alien—those things were huge.

I can recall many days, especially on Sundays, just wandering through the beauty parlor. I was so amazed at how those gas comb burners were made. I would often climb up and get on my knees in the chair to get a closer look at them; those little gas burners just amazed me.

But Aint Tee really did not like me in the beauty parlor. Often, she would scream from the back of the house, *"Boy!!!! Get out dat parlor ri'naw before you break som'un. You ain't 'pose to be in dere. Get out now!"*

Aint Tee was married a couple of times. Her last husband's first name was James. Uncle James is what we called him. Uncle James was a very dark complected, courteous, always jolly, and funny man. He was a seaman. He traveled the world on large ships as a deckhand. But when he was home, he kept the house incredibly clean. You could not find a speck of dirt on the floor when Uncle James was home, not that you could find dirt on the floor when he was not home. He was a great help to Aint Tee when he was home.

Uncle James loved to dance. He loved putting the radio on and dancing in the house. It was fun to watch him dance, especially when he would do the "Second Line" dance, which is the dance of New Orleans. I think I learned to do the Second Line by watching Uncle James. He would take that handkerchief out of his back pocket and Second Line as if he were the master of it, or as if he created the dance himself.

He also used to do this magic trick with a quarter. You know, the one where he shows you there is nothing in his hand, and then he puts his hand around the back of your head and pulls a quarter out. I still cannot figure out how he did that; he was fun.

My mom worked and sometimes Aint Tee would babysit or watch my sister and me. My sister and I would play out-side often while Aint Tee was taking care of her customers. One day, I got ahold of one of Aint Tee's hand mirrors and took it outside. Now, this was not just any ordinary kind of hand mirror. This was a special handheld mirror, trimmed in gold, and it had all types of costume jewelry glued on the back of it. It was her special mirror. Well, silly me got ahold of the mirror and took it outside and dropped it, breaking the glass mirror.

All I remember is hearing my sister say, *"Ooooooooooo! Ya gonna git it."*

I knew Aint Tee loved me; I never doubted it one day. I was her curly-headed, little Creole baby boy, but, that day, I think I was her worst nephew. True to my sister's words, I GOT IT. She literally tore my butt up; we were outside in front of the house, and everyone in that area of the village saw it. The neighbors did not know what was going on. All they heard was my aunt's voice describing why she was spanking me, and then they saw me screaming and crying. They probably thought she was killing me. She was so distressed and hysterical that day because of my breaking that mirror.

That was my first and only spanking I ever got from Aint Tee. I think she was more saddened about spanking me than she was about losing that mirror. I could not sit down for a week, joking!

The real estate/apartments Aint Tee owned were in the back of her house/beauty salon. We could hear and see people go in and out of the side-alley walkway all day and night. My great-grandmother Alma "Wilson" Levy, Grandma Alma, lived in one of the old servants' quarters in the back. That old lady would bathe my sister and me twice a day. She would not allow us to get too dirty.

There was this big concrete washtub connected to Aint Tee's house, in the backyard under this shaded roof. Grandma Alma was always back there with the radio tuned to the gospel station, washing clothes by hand with a scrub board. Sometimes I would sit on the steps or stoop off the back door and just watch her as I played around in the small area just outside the door or in the alleyway.

Usually, later in the day when she was ready to settle down for rest, Grandma Alma would get her a "cold one." Yes!! She would get one of the older gentlemen in the neighborhood to go to the corner store or bar to get her a bottle of beer. Falstaff, Jax, or Dixie beer, it did not matter. It was all good to her. Those three beer labels were local beer manufacturers in New Orleans back in the sixties.

Creole Meals

My sister and I would sleep with Grandma Alma sometimes in that back apartment—the old slave/servant quarters. It was funny because I still cannot figure out how the three of us slept in that little bed, in that little place.

When we would awaken for breakfast, you could smell the aroma of Grandma Alma and Aint Tee's favorite coffee, CDM's coffee and chicory. CDM stands for Café Du Monde. It is still sold today in a yellow package. Back then, it was only sold in a yellow canister. They would have that coffee good and hot every morning. And here is the best part; when Grandma Alma drank her coffee, her breakfast meal was French bread with thick butter spread on it. French bread is a traditional New Orleans long loaf of bread that is hard on the outside and soft on the inside. She would cut a piece for my sister and me, butter it down, and serve it to us with a cup of coffee with cream and sugar. We would dip the buttered French bread down into the coffee. It was unbelievably delicious.

Aint Tee would also cook flat cakes for breakfast. Flat cakes consisted of flour, water, egg, butter, and sugar mixed in a bowl and then poured onto a black skillet to fry. Once ready, those looked like pancakes, but were thicker and crispier on the outside than a pancake. Aint Tee and Grandma Alma would serve us those flat cakes with Brer Rabbit syrup, another old traditional type of food that New Orleanians preferred.

Aint Tee and Grandma were incredibly good cooks. Let me rephrase that; they were excellent cooks. Name it, they could cook it. One of the favorites was filé seafood gumbo that had shrimp, crabs, oysters, and an abundance of seasoning. Another favorite was Aint Tee's Camellia's red kidney beans, the gold standard, the world's best red beans. In my opinion, no one could cook red beans better than Aint Tee. We are not talking about Blue Runner's red beans; those are precooked canned beans.

I also remember eating fried fish with the fish head still on the fish. Grandma Alma and Aint Tee would scale the outside of the fish first, gut it down the middle, and then fry the fish still with the head on it. It was so good. Many days, when tenants who lived in the back apartments were walking through the alleyway while the cooking was going on, you would hear the person say, *"Som'un sho smells goooooood!"* The aroma of the food would flow out of the windows, into the alleyway, and throughout the neighborhood. Let us just say, no one I knew in the village had air-conditioning in the early sixties.

I remember what good neighbors Aint Tee and Grandma Alma were in that area of the village. They would give their leftover cooked food to people in the neighborhood, or to the people who lived in the back apartments, or to this gentleman, Jake, who lived across the street.

I can only describe Jake as a nice gentleman who hung out in the neighborhood every day, laughing and joking with people. Jake was a quiet, tall, dark complected, humble gentleman. He was Aint Tee's errand person. Jake's job was running errands in the neighborhood for everyone, and he was good at it. He would take trips to the grocery store for Aint Tee and Grandma Alma just about every day, and they would pay him well to do it. One day, I accompanied Jake on his trip to the corner store. He laughed and made fun of me all the way there because I had my shoes on wrong. He just thought that was the funniest thing he'd ever seen. He was a nice gentleman.

Aint Tee always wanted the best, and she, along with Grandma Alma, took excellent care of me and my sister. It seemed that my sister was Aint Tee's and Grandma's favorite, but that was far from the truth. Aint Tee and Grandma Alma would often purchase clothing for Dianne and help my mom with paying for Dianne's private-school education. I never felt bad about it, but I remember my mom one time mentioning, *"Y'all know, this boy needs clothes sometimes too?"* I was so young; it did not matter to me. As long as Aint Tee and Grandma Alma kept cooking and giving Dianne and me those flat cakes with syrup for breakfast, everything was okay with me.

As I grew and got my driver's license, Aint Tee made it her mission to take care of me financially. She never learned to drive, neither did most Black women in the sixties and before. I would drive her around to go shopping and/or pay the utility bills. I would take her on errands sometimes twice a week. She would give me five or ten dollars for driving her to different locations. MAN!!!!! Ten dollars a week was a lot of money back when I was in high school in 1974, '75, and '76.

Therefore, that spanking when I was three or four years old was all worth it. She was and is still deep in my memories and heart. I will always love and cherish Aint Tee and Grandma Alma. Love y'all.

The Circle Food Store, Lavata's Oyster House, and Chez Helene Restaurant

Sometimes we would walk from the apartment on Pauger Street to Aint Tee's house. On the walk there, we had to cross North Claiborne Avenue at Pauger Street. North Claiborne Avenue was one of the most beautiful streets in New

Orleans before the I-10 Interstate system came through Creole Village. I can remember many days walking down the middle of North Claiborne Avenue with my mom and sister during the hot summer. Those big oak trees that covered the median strip held back the hot sun.

Before the I-10 Interstate system, there was a concrete parking lot under the oak trees, across the street from Circle Food Store. Customers parked their cars in the parking lot in the median strip across the street from the Circle Food Store at the corner of North Claiborne Avenue and Saint Bernard Avenue.

Circle Food Store at the corner of Saint Bernard Avenue and North Claiborne.

Once you parked your car, Circle Food Store would provide shoppers with these square, red-colored, chest-high shopping carts on four wheels. They were about four feet tall, and we kids would hop or climb up on them and ride while someone pushed us.

My mom would let me ride on the bottom, and that was fun. Circle Food Store was a one-stop shopping experience. Customers could purchase all their grocery items, seafood, and meats, while having their prescriptions filled in the pharmacy. If you needed to see a doctor or dentist, they were located on the left side of the store; it was an awesome experience. Everyone in the place knew my mom and especially Aint Tee, because many of the ladies who worked there visited my aunt's beauty salon. The Circle Food Store was an exciting communal place where people just hung out all day, especially during the days preceding Easter.

Circle Food Store had shelving on the outside of the building, behind these large container doors. A couple of weeks before Easter, the employees would open the large container doors and fill the shelves with Easter candy and decorative Easter items. Everything you needed or wanted for Easter, from A to Z, could be found at Circle Food Store. That Circle Food Store Easter tradition continued for years, right up to Hurricane Katrina in 2005.

During Easter season, the store would also sell baby chicks. Why, you may ask. I have asked the same question in my older age. Why sell baby chickens during the Easter season, when the rabbit is associated with Easter? Not to cause confusion here, but have you ever seen a rabbit lay an egg? Anyway, my mother purchased a little chicken for us one time, and the poor thing died. As an adult parent, I purchased one for my kids some twenty-five years later. That poor thing died too.

Right next door to Circle Food Store, on North Claiborne Avenue, was a seafood restaurant and po'boy sandwich place called Lavata's Oyster House. This place had the best oysters in the city. Whether you wanted those fried or raw, Lavata's was the place to get your oysters, and especially your po'boy shrimp or oyster sandwich on French bread. I remember the place was always smoky and crowded with people, noon, evening, and late night. There were these green-colored wooden booths you had to sit in to be served, and the seats in those booths were hard wood.

This older White gentleman who managed the place was the conversation piece for everyone. I remember he wore these eyeglasses that were so thick I could not see his eyes when standing in front of him. Those glasses were so thick; we could not figure out how he could see out of them. I think he was half blind. This gentleman did not talk; he would only scream and shout all the time; he was a loud talker. We would just sit there and watch him as he interacted eccentrically with the customers; it was funny to see. Customers would start a conversation with him about anything, just to get him to scream so we all could laugh. He was a very funny character. Regardless, if you wanted the best oysters in New Orleans, Lavata's was the place; guaranteed, you would laugh and have a good time while dining in.

If you wanted good soul food other than Dooky Chase's, then right around the corner from Circle Food Store and Lavata's was Chez Helene. Chef Austin Leslie's cooking made Chez Helene a place to eat and socialize. Any type of soul food, fried chicken, red beans and rice, macaroni and cheese, smothered pork chops, etc.—it was there. My mom and dad were good friends with Chef Austin Leslie. We used to visit there often to eat, and Austin would come out to the table to sit and talk with us. I do not remember this personally, but it was told to me that many local civil rights planning meetings were held at Chez Helene, in addition to the meetings at Dooky Chase's. Chef Austin Leslie ended up catering my wedding some twenty years later.

On a stretch of North Claiborne Avenue, bounded by Basin/Orleans Avenues to the north and Elysian Fields Avenue to the south, this was a special place for Black people during the fifties, sixties, and early seventies. This area is presently still a gathering place on the weekends for urban millennials of New Orleans, but it now has a different social vibe. During my era, people would walk up and down this street all day and night; there was no crime. You could find all kinds of Black-owned businesses on North Claiborne Avenue: dress shops, shoe stores, barbershops, meat markets, bars, and funeral homes. Often, you would find older people just sitting outside and having a good time, sipping on their favorite beer or other drinks, talking and laughing; it seemed as if everyone knew each other. People were so polite and courteous back then. Even if they did not know you, everyone would respectfully say "good night" or "good evening" when walking by.

My sister and I were raised Catholic; therefore, I remember when my sister made her First Communion. After the ceremony, we walked along North Claiborne Avenue. She was still dressed in her white First Communion clothes, and as we visited with people who were sitting outside on their stoops, they would give my sister money just because she made her First Communion. More specifically, these folks would dig deep down into their pockets or purses to find a dime, ten cents, or as we called it in New Orleans, a "silver dime."

This tradition of giving little children a silver dime was an extremely popular First Communion ritual in New Orleans, or at least on North Claiborne Avenue. Legend said back then that if you collected many dimes on your First Communion, it would bring you good luck. I remember walking with my sister the day she made her First Communion, and she collected tons of silver dimes. I could not wait to make my First Communion. I needed some good luck too, as you will read later in this book. The picture on the front of this book, with my sister and I, was taken on the day of my sister's First Communion; my mom dressed me in white to walk with her.

My Dad's Bar—Two Brothers

My dad operated a bar two blocks off North Claiborne Avenue in the Seventh Ward. It was called Two Brothers, and it was on the corner of Saint Anthony Street and North Roman Streets. This bar was only two blocks up the street and one block around the corner from Aint Tee's home. My dad—or Slim, as the locals called him—and his brother James, also known as Chink, owned and managed the bar, a sweet-shop/candy store, and an apartment complex.

My dad's barroom, Two Brothers, on the corner of Saint Anthony Street and North Roman Street. It probably had new owners when it was destroyed by Katrina and later demolished by the City of New Orleans.

Two Brothers was the happening spot for Creole people. My dad had a daughter, an older sister of mine with whom I never visited. She lived in Los Angeles, California. We talked on the phone a couple of times, and she said that Cab Calloway, when visiting New Orleans during the late forties and early fifties, would hang out at my dad's bar. That is similar to Michael Jackson or Beyoncé visiting a bar today. That is how famous Cab Calloway was back in those days.

Cab Calloway visited my dad's bar. My father is the gentleman
on the left, or to Cab's right. Cool cats. Watch out ladies!

No telling how many other famous Black musicians and actors visited my dad's bar back then because it was one of the hot spots in the village. Music was always blaring from the juke box in the bar. I can hear Fats Domino's "Blueberry Hill" in my head as I write this book, and Frogman Henry's "Ain't Got No Home."

On Mardi Gras Day, the Mardi Gras Indians would stop at my dad's bar to get their alcoholic refreshments—"fire water" is what they called it.

On Mardi Gras Day, local African American males
masquerade in Native American clothing.

Several years later, before Hurricane Katrina, I was told by world-renowned and famous Chef Austin Leslie, that my dad had one of the biggest gambling hot spots in the Seventh Ward, and even the policemen, both White and Black, would be in the back of the bar, gambling and visiting with the ladies upstairs. I always wondered why policemen were constantly at my dad's bar, just about every time I went there. One day, I remember visiting my dad's bar, and there were several White police officers in the place just hanging out.

One cop asked my dad, *"Hey, Slim, is dat cha boy?"*

"Yeah," my dad responded.

Then all the policeman laughed.

I never figured out why those policemen were laughing until I was an older adult. They laughed because they had concluded, just by observing my physical appearance, that Slim had fathered a child with a Black woman. I have no idea why that was so funny. Maybe I did not understand the culture of the fifties and sixties as well back then as I think I do now.

My father was probably paying the policemen under the table to keep his bar open because my dad had money falling out of his pockets. He always had rolls of money stuffed in his pants pockets. He would reach down and easily pull out a roll of one-hundred-dollar bills. My dad would buy a new Cadillac every two or three years. Those big, pointed lights on the backs of those vehicles always amazed me, and I was always elated when he would take me for a ride in the "Big Kitty Cat."

Chapter 11

Growing in Knowledge

The Years of Innocence

While finishing my undergrad degree at the age of thirty-six, I had to take a public-speaking class. The first day in class, we had to stand up and tell our life history for ten minutes. This was the professor's way of evaluating our speaking and articulation abilities. Well, I did not know that for thirty-six years I had been speaking incorrectly, mispronouncing words, and using incorrect diction.

When I started my speech that night in class, I opened by saying, *"Hi, I ma Herman Galatas, and I ma from the Nigh Ward."* The speech professor looked up, stopped me at that point, and asked that I repeat my introduction. So I did and continued speaking. I did not know what to make of the situation, but I was open to constructive criticism.

Basically, to make a long story short about that terrible verbal speech, that was the best thing that has ever happened in my life. After class that night, the professor told me my grade for that speech was an F. I was shocked. It blew me away. But she continued with her constructive criticism with words of encouragement. We sat down and talked for about another fifteen minutes, and she gave me the A to Z's about public speaking. She said, in her opinion, perhaps one of the reasons I may have been held back from career advancement was the way I spoke.

"Y'all know som'un? She whaz righ!" Before that, I hadn't been able to figure out, for the last twelve years of my career,

why I was achieving quotas and performing outstanding on my job, but was continually overlooked every time a promotion came up. No one on my job was brave enough to tell me I had terrible verbal communication skills.

From that night on, I accepted the challenge and immediately corrected my speaking and writing skills. It took me three hard years of consistent mental alertness to change thirty-six years of incorrect pronunciations/articulation. I still have a small problem with correction diction/articulation today, but it is one hundred percent better. Oh, I passed that class with a B!

Point here is that knowledge and learning never stop!!!! And starting with this chapter, my knowledge and cognitive development of my world is just beginning.

My Grandparents

In 1961/1962, we moved from the Pauger Street location in the Seventh Ward to the Desire Housing Project in the Ninth Ward. The Desire Housing Project was about a half mile from where my grandmother Valetta lived. We did not call Valetta Grandma or Maw-Maw; I don't know why. We called her Mama. Strange, I know, but we loved it. My step-grandfather, Valetta's husband, was Gilbert. We did not call him Grandpa or Paw-Paw. We called him Daddy. Strange, I know, but we were all happy with it.

Valetta and Gilbert had another daughter, Melva, my mom's baby sister. She was ten years older than I was, and seven years older than my sister. So, Dianne and I never called Melva Aint-Tee or aunt Melva because we basically grew up together; we just called her Melva.

My sister and I were at my grandmother's home often.

Desire Housing Project, Ninth Ward, New Orleans, Louisiana. We lived here from 1962 to 1966.

Clouet Street, Desire Community, and the Ninth Ward

Valetta and Gilbert had a genuinely nice, small two-bedroom house with a big yard on Clouet Street, just down from George Washington Carver High School and Saint Philip the Apostle Catholic Elementary School. They also had a dog named Spike, and he was one hundred percent collie. Valetta was a stay-at-home mom; Gilbert was a seaman, like my uncle James. But Gilbert was a cook, not a deckhand like uncle James, on the big cargo ships that went abroad for months at a time. Gilbert would bring back all types of nice jewelry, electronics, and furniture from his travels. Gilbert and Valetta were the first Black people in their neighborhood to have a color TV.

My grandmother, Valetta Levy Moore Pratts.

I remember watching that big, nice color TV often with Melva. The local dance program that aired on Saturday afternoons on channel 4WWL was Melva's favorite, *The John Pela Show*. We would enjoy all the songs and try to mimic the dance steps in the living room. Melva also loved the radio. I was introduced to all the sixties music by Melva, and she is the reason, to this day, that I am a Beatles and Motown fan.

On Friday nights, the horror movies would air on TV. There we were, camped out in front of the big color TV, ready to watch Morgus the Magnificent. Morgus was a crazy scientist who would present the featured horror movie of the week. Morgus had an assistant named Chopsley. Chopsley was tall and wore a dark-brown Grim Reaper outfit that scared me to death. I would sit there in front of the TV, scared to my bones, and Melva and Dianne would laugh the entire time.

They were silly girls, and the only good thing about watching those horror movies is that it kept Melva's and Dianne's minds off tying me down in a chair and putting ribbons in my curly brown hair, which is something they would often do. They thought I was so cute with that curly hair, so they would tie me down in a chair and put girly ribbons in my hair. I guess they wished my mom would have had another girl instead of a boy. I do not hate them for it. My mom and grandmother would scream at them to stop whenever they caught those two doing this to me.

My mom really detested it. She would scream at the top of her lungs, *"Melva and Dianne, get dem ribbons out dat boy hair. He ain't no girl, and I ain't raisin' no sissy."*

Gilbert, My Stepgrandfather

Gilbert, my stepgrandfather, was the joy and pride of my life. Again, we called him Daddy, and he loved it. He would take me fishing and crabbing and do all the things grandfathers were accustomed to doing. He purchased every bike I ever possessed up until I went to college; that was the last one. He would wrestle and shadowbox with me on the front lawn when I was young, or on the floor in the living room sometimes. He gave me my nickname: Dirty Red. Whenever I came in the house with dirty clothes on after playing outside, he would call over to me, *"Hey, Dirty Red."* That name stuck around even when I was clean. As I got older, he just called me Red.

Desire Housing Project nursery, 1962. To the right of the older gentleman, I am the second person and am in a bow tie and checkered jacket.

Hand Burning—Mercy and Grace

When I was three or four years old, I was in the backyard with Gilbert, cutting grass. Well, let us just say, he was cutting the grass with the lawnmower, and I was watching him. On this day when he was cutting grass in the backyard on Clouet Street, he stopped the lawnmower and started working on something else in the backyard. I, out of curiosity, concentrated on this bright, glowing-red pipe sticking out of the side of the lawnmower. I did not ever remember seeing that pipe so red and glowing so brightly; that pipe was always a dark brown when the lawnmower was off and parked under the house. I puzzled over it, but I just could not figure out how that pipe got so red and glowing. I walked over, stopped at the lawnmower, and looked at the bright-red, glowing pipe, still trying to figure out how that dark-brown pipe became bright red. Gilbert was off in the distance doing something else and not paying much attention to what I was about to do.

So, as a three or four-year-old kid, not able to figure out mentally how that pipe turned red, I decided to touch it to see if I could find the answer to the question. I bent over, reached down, and grabbed the pipe. Immediately, I found out why the pipe was red. *"Ahhhhh!!!!"* I screamed as if it were the end of the world. That pipe was hot as hell. No, I am wrong. It was hotter than hell. I was jumping up and down, crying and screaming while holding my hand.

I believe one of my angels, Mercy or Grace, pulled my hand off the pipe, because the pipe was so hot my hand should have stuck to it and been braised. I could have lost my hand or arm.

Gilbert turned around from what he was doing and ran to my rescue. He could not believe what was happening because I was always right within his reach. My grandmother and mom came out of the house frantically, looked at me, and started crying hysterically, trying to figure out what to do. Gilbert was so scared for me I remember his crying too; he thought it was his fault that his little Dirty Red's right palm was scorched with burn marks. My mom called my dad, and it was a good thing she did. I had second-degree burns on the palm of my right hand, and I was just a three or four-year-old baby.

Earlier, I mentioned to you that I thought my dad passed for White, but I had no evidence to prove it at the time. This situation is one of the reasons I can definitively conclude my dad passed for White sometimes. My dad knew a lot of people throughout New Orleans, professional and not. He also carried a New Orleans policeman's badge, so he had a little clout.

My dad came over to the house after my mom called him, and he took me to a White doctor's office in the middle of the Central Business District (CBD), across the street from the New Orleans Public Service Inc. (NOPSI) at 916 Union Street. We all know that in 1961/62, Black people did not go to a doctor's office in Downtown CBD, New Orleans; however, my dad took me to the CBD to see a doctor. He may have known the doctor personally or as a patient, because the doctor took me in right away. To this day, I still wonder how my dad knew that doctor.

The doctor and his staff took really good care of this little Creole boy. On that first visit, the doctor took me in and performed a miracle on my burned hand. He applied some type of medication, wrapped it up, and gave my dad some medication to apply. The doctor's diagnosis, examination, and treatment were so astonishing that I never had a permanent burn scar. On my follow-up visits to the office, the two "yellow-haired" nurses would pick me up while sitting at their desks, sit me on their laps, and give me candy, show me magazines and books, read to me, and walk with me outside while my dad and the doctor discussed my continuing treatments and return appointments. I thought I was in heaven. When it was time to leave, those nurses would stuff all my pockets with more candy. They were sincerely amazing and wonderful people. Hopefully, God blessed them throughout their years of living for taking good care of me.

My right hand eventually healed. My grandfather Gilbert was glad that my dad intervened and got the proper attention for my burned hand. He had his Dirty Red back, and my hand was healed. We could go fishing and crabbing again.

Saint Philip the Apostle Catholic Elementary School

My sister and I attended Saint Philip the Apostle Elementary School right up the street from Valetta and Gilbert's house on Clouet Street. Now that I am older, I understand why the principal of the school, Sister Rhomonda, a White nun, was so fond of me. Sister Rhomonda, or as we called her, Mother Rhomonda, was a very fair-complected, middle-aged White nun with a round face. I can't explain anymore of her physical appearance because the nun's habit was so long that it covered her shoes, and the bonnet was so tight on her head that the veins on her forehead stuck out.

My mom would say, *"If mothda Rhomonda would have had a kid, she wish it would looked like you."*

Mother Rhomonda thought I was the cutest little kindergarten boy she ever saw. Just before school would let out every day, she would call me to the school office on the intercom system and ask me to carry her office bag to the nun's residence where she lived. I often looked forward to those afternoon walks because I got out of class, and those walks were very enjoyable. She was a pleasant lady. After I would carry or tug along that heavy bag, she would give me cookies and punch or some type of candy. Those treats after carrying that heavy bag made the experience even more memorable. One time, believe it or not, she had some marbles she had taken away from some of the kids at school. So she and I played a marble game on the floor in the nun's residence while eating cookies and drinking punch.

I cannot understand why, out of all the students, she picked me. I honestly do not believe she discriminated against anyone else by showing me favoritism because of my skin complexion. I honestly believe I was not one of her favorites because of skin color because I remember her getting some of the older, darker-complected kids to carry her bag when it was too heavy for me. I remember getting jealous one time when I saw another kid carrying her bag, and I wanted to beat him up. I could not wait for my name to be called across the intercom. I will never forget that nice nun. I am sure there must be a special place for her in heaven.

While in kindergarten at Saint Philip's, we had a Christmas play. All the kids in kindergarten had to dress up in different costumes, and my mom dressed me up like a doctor in my child's doctor costume. There was a TV program at the time called *Dr. Ben Casey*, so I dressed up as Dr. Ben Casey, a doll doctor. We had to march across the stage, like toy soldiers, to the music of *The Nutcracker*. Every time I hear that song during the holidays, I remember that Christmas play as if it were yesterday.

A year later during first grade, I had to perform on that same stage at Saint Philip's. There was a talent show, and somehow my sister and her friends made me and this other first-grader dance in it. What dance did we do, you ask? What other dance were Black kids doing in the early sixties? The James Brown. Just as Michael Jackson did when he and his brothers auditioned for Motown. That was a big thing back then among teenagers and adults—to get little kids to dance like the R&B singer James Brown.

I remember trying to outdance my friend while onstage, but he was cutting the stage floor better than I was. While performing the James Brown dance, he proceeded to take off his jacket, as James Brown would do, and he tossed his jacket into the crowd of spectators; the little girls in the audience started screaming, mimicking a real James Brown concert, which was fun.

My Mom's Big Black Car and Kid with Yellow Hair

I enjoyed listening to James Brown on the radio in my mom's big black car. That car was so big and roomy on the inside that Dianne and I would fall asleep on the back seat, and there was still enough room for maybe two or three more kids to sleep. My mom used to drive us all around the city in that car, not just to other Black neighborhoods, but all over the city—uptown, downtown, mid-city, Chalmette, Lakefront, all over. We would just ride many days, and my mom would take her time and educate us about the different locations, neighborhoods, schools, and buildings. Thanks to my mom, Dianne and I were deeply knowledgeable young kids when it came to our community and the surrounding areas of New Orleans.

One day while riding in the back seat of the car, I remember passing through a White neighborhood in the Eighth Ward on Florida Avenue around McCue Playground, approaching Almonaster Boulevard. From the back seat of the car, I saw this little kid outside playing, and he had yellow hair, similar to that of the nurses in the doctor's office where my father took me when I burned my hand. As I was looking at this kid from the back seat of the car, I remembered those nice nurses with their yellow hair, so I screamed to my sister, *"Dianne! Looka dat boy wit yella hair!"* I remember that day as if it were yesterday, but, more importantly, I remember my mom and Dianne's reactions to that statement. They started laughing so uncontrollably that we almost got into an automobile accident.

I was not laughing. I could not understand what was so funny. All I did was describe what I saw. A White kid with yellow hair, right? So, what was so funny? I just stood there on the back floor of the car, with my hands and arms hanging down over the top of the front seat, watching those two continue to laugh.

They eventually stopped laughing, and that was the day I learned the description and definition of blonde hair. The phrase "blonde hair" was not part of my vocabulary yet because I'd never heard anyone use it to describe someone's hair. I did not feel bad about the correction because my mom and sister were always teaching and correcting me about issues or situations I had no idea about, and I trusted their explanations about everything. Their explanations, teachings, and information were gospel to me. So if they said it, it was true. On that day, they educated me about blonde hair. One thing I knew for sure: I had never seen blonde or yellow hair in the ghetto where we lived. Never. So how was I supposed to know yellow hair was called blonde?

On another occasion while my mom was driving us around in that big black car, we were riding east through the Seventh Ward on Hope Street, heading back home towards the Ninth Ward. I was lying down on the back seat of the car, and my mom called out to me to get up and look out the window.

I could hear musical instruments, like horns and drums, coming from somewhere while we passed through that neighborhood, but I could not see where the music was coming from. She kept driving several more feet; then my mom veered to the right side of the street and parked the car behind this big fence. I looked out of the car's window, and there they were—the Marching 100.

The Saint Augustine Catholic High School and Marching 100

Saint Augustine's (Saint Aug) is an all-boy, predominantly Black, Catholic high school that was built in the 1950s. This school, especially during the civil rights struggles in the fifties and sixties, was the pride of the Black community. Many Black students who attended Saint Aug have gone on to very productive, accountable, professional careers in politics, law, business, music, and sports.

The Marching 100 is the official name of Saint Augustine's marching band. On that day, when we were passing by, they were practicing in Saint Aug's field yard. This was before the basketball gym was built on campus; therefore, the yard was big, and the band had enough room to spread out and strut their stuff.

Saint Augustine Catholic High School, New Orleans, Louisiana.

We stopped to watch, and we were not the only ones; there were about forty to sixty people standing, dancing, and watching the band as they practiced in the yard. I remember watching those band members as they marched up and down that yard, rocking those bass drums from side to side, blowing those horns, and blowing them loudly. I thought to myself, *Man, those boys are cool*, and I wished I could do that one day.

Well, band practice ended, and my mom, my sister, and I got back into the car and continued on our journey.

Canal Street and Mr. Bingle

The Saint Augustine Marching 100 band was one the coolest things to watch as a young kid, but the Marching 100 had major competition for my attention during the Christmas holidays because my favorite thing to watch then was Mr. Bingle.

Mr. Bingle was an animated Christmas character that wore a big upside-down snow cone with a red stocking on his head. He, several other characters, and a Christmas village were displayed in the big front windows of the Maison Blanche building, a major clothing retailer on Canal Street.

Maison Blanche on Canal Street, Roman Chewing Candy
cart in foreground, and Mr. Bingle on building, 1970s.

Mr. Bingle only came out during the Christmas season. Many of us kids, would stand there in front of the Maison Blanche building and look at the Christmas village through the store window. Mr. Bingle was always placed in the center of the Christmas village. Like all small kids, I was intrigued with the small toy train that rolled around in a circle under the Christmas tree and throughout the Christmas village. Mr. Bingle would fly back and forth on a string above the village, and his mouth would move up and down as his voice came out of speakers above, wishing everyone a "Merry Christmas and a Happy New Year." Mr. Bingle was one of those New Orleans-created characters that many people my age enjoyed as a young kid.

Krauss and Canal Street

When it was not Christmas, it was still an adventure to go to Canal Street to shop, especially at Krauss. As a young kid, on a couple of occasions, my dad took me to Krauss. That was the only time he and I had quality time together, other than when I visited with him at his bar. You could buy anything at Krauss: clothing, jewelry, toys, furniture, and even dine in at the café. Everyone who grew up in New Orleans before the eighties probably shopped at Krauss on Canal Street at least one time.

The old Krauss Building on Canal Street, New Orleans, Louisiana.

From my five or six-year-old observation, and even up to my adult years, I thought some of the nicest people ever placed on planet Earth worked at Krauss. Genuinely nice and personable, and it seemed that everyone, regardless of race or religioin, while in Krauss was very respectful of each other. Krauss was a place were everyone felt and was treated as equal, based on my personal experiences every time I went shopping with Mama Valetta and Aint Tee as a small kid.

Krauss employees honored prices, even when those prices were wrong. On one of my shopping experiences when I was a sophomore in high school, during the fall of 1973, I went to Krauss to purchase some bell-bottom blue jeans. I grabbed some expensive blue jeans off the table, and those were marked one dollar. I could not believe it—one dollar!. So I asked the sales-lady, *"Ma'am, dees jeans really one dollar?"*

She asked to see the tag, looked at me, smiled, and told me that, while marking those jeans down from twelve dollars to ten, she'd apparently forgotten to place a zero behind the one on the yellow tag. Therefore, she said it was her mistake, and she sold those jeans to me for one dollar. Those were the kind of people who worked at Krauss: good, honest people.

I wore those jeans to school three to four days a week during my sophomore year of high school and to Friday-night football games. Best dollar I ever spent.

Rosie

Another New Orleans-created, animated character I and so many other New Orleanians were fascinated with was Rosie.

She was on the front window of Rosenberg's Furniture on Tulane

Avenue. Rosenberg's used to run a local TV commercial in which the animated character Rosie—adorned with black hair, red dress, white socks, and black shoes—would sing. Every time we passed that store in my mom's big black car, my sister and I would sing the Rosie song. You would have to be from New Orleans to know the jingle, but it got plenty of airtime up until the early eighties. You may want to ask the Hip Hop Rapper from New Orleans, Lil Wayne, about this song.

Schwegmann Giant Super Markets

Rosenberg's was a major furniture retailer in New Orleans for many years until the middle eighties, but when it came to groceries, the best grocery shopping trips were those to Schwegmann Giant Super Markets in Gentilly, a neighborhood in New Orleans.

Schwegmann Brothers Giant Super Markets, their old building on Old Gentilly Road. The car off the road is getting gas.

This building was so gigantic, as a small kid, you could literally get lost in the building. Schwegmann, to the best of my understanding, was the first grocery "superstore" of its kind in the world. It had a jewelry store, a clothing store, a shoe store, a shoe-repair store, a cleaners, a pharmacy, a café/deli, and a seafood market; for me, the best areas of the store were the toy and pet stores upstairs.

It even had a check-cashing area where people could also pay their utility bills—water, gas, electric, and phone bill. During that period, people did not have checking accounts, so they couldn't mail in bill payments. You had to go to the water, gas, or electric building, NOPSI, New Orleans Public Service, Incorporated on Carondelet Street. To pay your phone bill, you went right up the street to the Bell South building. Thanks to Schwegmann for making the one-stop experience efficient for everyone's needs. Oh!!!! Outside, there was even a gas station.

Before the seventies, people did not go shopping in just any type of clothing. People literally dressed up. Men wore dress slacks and a shirt, no jeans. Ladies dressed up in skirts, carried their big purses, and wore hats. Going shopping was a big dress-up occasion.

Whenever we went shopping at the Schwegmann location in Gentilly, as soon as we entered the store, I would take off for the toy and pet stores. Sometimes, I would just walk all around by myself in that humongous store while my mom shopped. When my mom was finished, she would go to Customer Service and have my name called over the intercom because she knew I was running around somewhere in the building. That was okay back then. I was not the only kid in the toy and pet stores, nor the only kid running around while their parents were shopping. Those other parents, when they finished shopping, had to have their children's names announced over the intercom too.

Chapter III

The Awakening

Racism, Society, and God

Am I Different?

On one Christmas Day while we were living in the Desire Housing Project around 1963/64, it seemed as if every kid and teenager wanted or got a pair of skates on Christmas morning. We lived on one of the main streets in the Desire Housing Project, Alvar Street. This street was nice and smooth, and on Christmas Day, our street was packed like sardines in a can. Young people were skating up and down the street, dancing, singing, and just having fun on Christmas Day. You could not find an open spot in the street to skate freely; there were that many kids out there.

On that Christmas Day, at the age of five or six, I was "awakened" to the fact that my skin complexion was a little different from many of the other people and family members I was around every day. My sister and I received a pair of skates on Christmas morning, and we wanted to go outside to skate with the other kids, so we did just that.

My sister and I took off rolling down the crowded street, not bothering anyone and especially trying not to bump into anyone. We literally were just concentrating on staying balanced to keep from falling off the skates and breaking a leg or ankle.

Then I hear some kids yelling, *"Hey!!!!! Looka da White boy tryin' da skate."*

I did not know about whom they were talking. I knew I was not White, so to whom could they be referring? I turned around, and, the next thing I knew, my sister was about to fight with one of the kids who'd shouted because she knew they were referring to, and making fun of, me.

My sister would never back down from a fight, whether to defend herself or me. I would not call her a fighter, nor would she be the first to start a fight, but if she had to defend herself or me, you better put your money on my sister, "Big Dee." My sister always—I repeat, always—came to my defense.

On this Christmas day, she came to her little, light-skinned baby brother's defense again. In a very loud and unfriendly scream, my sister shouted back at those kids, *"Hey, he ain't no White boy—he my broda."*

All those kids just stood there and said nothing; no one retaliated. They knew who had just spoken—Big Dee. None of those kids were about to start trouble, not on Christmas Day and not with Big Dee!

We turned around and went on our merry way to finish skating. It turned out to be a very nice Christmas day, and no one got into an altercation.

Hey, White boy!

While living in the Desire Housing Project, Dianne and I attended Saint Philip's Catholic Elementary School. One day, I was walking home from school through the Desire Housing Project. I can't remember the exact grade—first or second—but I do remember this incident as if it were yesterday.

It was springtime, and kids around my age were sitting on the steps in the back area of the project and playing in the driveways throughout the streets. As I walked through the area, they started shouting viciously at me.

"Hey, White boy!"

"Hey, White boy!"

"Hey, looka da White boy!"

I stopped and stood there, not knowing what was about to happen next. My response was *"I ain't no White boy."*

They started approaching and surrounding me while saying, *"Yeah, you is a White boy."*

I kept repeating, *"I ain't no White boy,"* but that was not good enough.

They would not accept my response and decided to physically beat me up.

An elderly woman screamed from her window, *"Y'all stop dat; y'all stop dat; stop beatin' dat boy up."*

Somehow, I got away and ran home fast. Still crying, I told my sister what happened.

Revenge Is Mine, Sayeth Big Dee!!!

Dianne and I returned to the place I got beat up, and we saw those same kids sitting on the steps. Dianne went into her revenge attitude. She started approaching those kids without asking a question, then proceeded to physically fight with one or two of them.

That same elderly lady, who earlier screamed at those kids to stop beating up on me, was now cheering Dianne on to kick their little butts. It was fun to watch those boys run away crying like little babies. I never again had a problem walking through that part of the project after school.

The Woods

Some of those same kids, who were overzealous about my being White, lived in and around our area, and they roamed through the different areas of the projects every day. These kids sometimes would venture into areas where we were not permitted to go, areas that were off-limits.

One of those was a large wooded tract directly across the street from where we lived. Many of the kids who lived in the projects would go walking through those woods, which was extremely dangerous because we were warned by the authorities and local adults that the area contained perilous insects and poisonous snakes.

I had gone in those woods once or twice with other kids, but on this particular day I did not. My sister, some friends, and I were sitting outside on the steps that led up to our apartment. We were just hanging out, playing and goofing around as children do. Unexpectedly, we saw some kids coming out of the woods talking loudly and laughing. One of them had a long stick in his hand, and he was holding the stick far out in front of his body. Wrapped around that stick was a light-green snake. While walking towards us, the boy holding the stick was teasing his friends by poking the snake on the stick towards them. Kids were screaming and running everywhere, scared as hell. As he got closer to us, I just stood there and watched. Believe it or not, I got up close to the stick to get a better look.

But this was a bad situation for my poor sister. Big Dee was tough when it came down to fighting or protecting us, but she was painstakingly frightened by any kind of insect or small creature. These kids already knew Big Dee would be terrified if they could get near her with the snake. On a previous occasion, they had chased her around the project's buildings with a gar, a long, thin fish with sharp teeth; so, revenge for them was to scare the hell out of her with this snake.

As they got closer, Dianne started screaming and hollering at the top of her lungs, and running everywhere while they pursued her, poking the snake towards her. There was nothing little me could do because I was afraid of the snake too. She probably could have had a heart attack that day and died because she was in a screaming fury.

Revenge is ours, sayeth those kids!

I Almost Drowned—Mercy and Grace

Before you entered that same wooded area where those kids found that green snake, there was a drainage canal that had a muddy embankment on both sides of the ten- to twelve-foot-deep ditch. When it rained, the water from the streets would drain into this canal and go underground.

One Sunday afternoon, my mom had some friends visiting, and I asked if I could go outside to play. I happened to be dressed neatly, so my mother cautiously warned me not to get dirty. Before allowing me to go outside and play, my mother also told me, as she usually did, to stay away from the woods and that canal. On this day, I did not follow those instructions.

As soon as I went outside, and for some strange reason, I started heading directly to the drainage canal. That was odd because no other person, kid or adult, was outside, nor was there anyone observing out of their windows, which was common in the hood. There I stood, on the grassy, muddy embankment of the canal, looking down and watching the water drain into the large pipe flowing underground. I found it fascinating, so I just stood there watching. I started walking along the muddy embankment and looked down to pick up a stick to throw into the canal. Suddenly, I lost my balance, slipped, fell on my side and stomach, and started sliding down the muddy embankment into the canal.

I tried to reach for anything I could grab on to as I was sliding down feet first into the water. I was reaching for something to hold on to, to keep from slipping down the muddy embankment when suddenly I saw to my right a tree root sticking out of the muddy embankment. It was not just any type of tree root. It was shaped like a *U*, or a horseshoe, and was sticking out of the muddy embankment to the right of my body. With nothing under my feet as I kept sliding down, I grabbed hold of that U-shaped root with my right hand and held on for dear life.

As I am dangling there, I could hear my mother's voice in the back of my mind, "*Stay away from dat drainage canal.*" Somehow, I held on to that root with all my might, dragged my right leg up over it, and pulled myself up out of that muddy drainage canal. Alleluia, amazing!

Somewhere in the genetic makeup of that tree, there was a DNA code that instructed it to produce a U-shaped root that would stick out of the muddy embankment and hang there like a rope for me to grabbed on to. *WOW!* Somehow, that root was strong enough to hold my weight, and I was given the muscle strength that allowed me to pull myself up out of that canal. I know my two angels, Mercy and Grace, were there with me that day too. I am sure they helped by pushing me up that embankment.

I was extremely scared to face my mother, but I went home anyway, with ninety percent of the front of my body covered in mud and grass. When I entered the house, my mom looked at me with a frown on her face, and she wasn't happy. I had come home with mud on my clothes in front of her friends. What she did not know was that she almost lost her little, curly-headed baby boy; he almost drowned in that drainage canal. She asked how my clothes had gotten so muddy, and I wondered whether or not to tell her the truth. I ended up saying that I was playing close to the wooded area, but not actually in the woods, and that there was a muddy area on the ground, into which I slipped. Well, that was kind of what happened. I surely did not tell her I fell into the drainage canal and almost drowned. I guess something told me to protect my mom's emotions that day, or maybe I just wanted to save my butt.

Summer Camp, Lincoln Beach, Abita Springs, Louisiana, and the Pool

I may have missed my opportunity to swim in that drainage canal, but to cool off in the summertime, the Catholic priest at Saint Philip's Church/School would take the kids who attended summer camp swimming. Whenever the other kids who lived in the projects, the ones who never attended summer camp, heard that the camp attendees were going swimming, they would show up and try to get on the bus. It often caused confusion, but somehow the camp directors always worked it out. The Priest would take us across Lake Pontchartrain to a small community called Abita Springs. There was a park located in Abita Springs.

Dianne and I would go to Abita Springs, and Lincoln Beach with the local Baptist church too. One of our neighbors who lived in the same complex was a pastor. Every year, his church would have a picnic. We did not attend his church, but because we were neighbors, he always invited us. So, we'd pack a picnic basket and go off to Lincoln Beach or Abita Springs. Those were the good old days.

In Abita Springs, there was this large public park that had a big swimming pool. It was the only public pool I knew of back in the early sixties, outside of city limits, that allowed Black folks to swim. This pool was not square, like traditional pools, but round like a circle. It seemed as if it took me all day to walk around that big pool. Round and round and round all day. The Black folks had a good time there.

During segregation, before integration, Lincoln Beach, on the east side of Lake Pontchartrain, at the end of Haynes Boulevard, was where Black folks enjoyed their summertime recreation. I can remember the pool and the grandstand. Entertainers like Little Richard, Fats Domino, and many others would occasionally perform on that stage, but I was only interested in the pool and the beach.

One year, my mom really surprised Dianne and me with a big announcement. For our summer vacation, we were going to Miami Beach.

Vacation—Miami Beach

My mom came to us one summer day in 1965 and told us we were taking a driving vacation, and that vacation was going to be a visit to Miami Beach, Florida. I was seven years old; I didn't know one thing about Miami Beach. I didn't know where Miami Beach was or how to get there. All I knew was that we were leaving home, staying in a hotel with a swimming pool, and visiting the beach in a place called Miami. That was okay with me.

My mom had a friend with a strange name—Tatel. Her skin was very fair, maybe lighter than mine. I thought she was White. My mom's friend brought her niece Kate along on the trip too, so it was three kids and two adults off to Miami. My mom's friend was a very nice lady, and she liked my sister and me; we liked her too. I think Ms. Tatel was very successful, but I never knew her occupation or if she inherited money. She lived in a big, beautiful house uptown, one block from Ferret Street, and she drove a new 1964 or 1965 Deuce and a Quarter, a Buick Electra 225. At the time, it was considered a state-of-the-art vehicle. It had all the accessories—air-conditioning, power seats, power windows, a radio, you name it. It had everything a seven-year-old kid could want, other than a bathroom.

We took off for Miami early one summer morning in 1965. I remember passing through Mobile, Alabama, and seeing White folks in other cars. They were looking at us as if we were strangers from a foreign land. I slept most of the time, and when we got to Panama City, Florida, in the panhandle, I asked my mom if we could stop because out of the car window I had seen several amusement parks with rides and swimming pools. She said no, without any further explanation. I kept persisting and crying, to the point that I aggravated my mom's friend.

Those roller coasters and other rides looked fun. They seemed better than the ones at Lincoln Beach. Other than Lincoln Beach, which is bordered on Lake Pontchartrain with brown sand, I had never seen a theme park or amusement park with such gigantic rides, or such beautiful green-blue water and white, sandy beaches. As I was watching all those kids out there having fun, I wanted to do the same.

My mom kept telling me, *"We can't; we can't; we can't stop!"*

I really didn't understand why we couldn't stop the car, go up to a ride, buy a ticket, and get on the ride. Well, my mom eventually gave into my annoying cries and decided to explain to her seven-year-old son why we could not go out onto that beautiful white, sandy beach and enjoy those wonderful rides.

Now, I am about to get my first explanation about racism. My mom started by saying, *"Dem people don't like people like us. We can't go play with dem."*

I was seven years old at the time, and I have never forgotten that. There were signs that read, "No Colors Allowed." It was my first lesson in racial discrimination, but I still did not fully comprehend it yet. Honestly, before that trip to Miami, I guess I was too young to comprehend racism. At home, to best of my knowledge, we had never visited places that discriminated, at least not yet.

When we arrived in Miami, believe it or not, we stayed at the fabulous Fontainebleau Hotel. That is the same hotel where Dorothy Dandridge performed in the late fifties and where she had to stay in a room behind the kitchen during her engagement. And there we were, in that big luxury hotel and with accommodations on one of the upper floors.

As kids, we could not enjoy the hotel the way the adults enjoyed it because the place was so big. We kept getting lost every time we went down to the pool, so the adults decided to find us a more family-oriented hotel on the beach. We ended up at a small motel, and it was very nice. We kids could go in and out of the room, run or walk back and forth to the pool and to the beach without supervision.

So now, we were starting to have a good time, to the point where one of us almost drowned.

My Sister Almost Drowned

On this hot, sunny day, we all went out to the pool, which was packed with families vacationing from all over, especially from the North. Everyone was having a good time, and we were treated as equals at this motel. There was a small tavern/bar poolside, where adults could get drinks, and a barbecue pit, where someone was in fact smoking food, so it was a good vacation day for all the people who were staying at the motel.

I was in the pool, playing with some other kids. I didn't know where any of my family members, my mom's friend, or her niece were because we were all in a safe environment, and everyone was off doing their own thing. I couldn't swim, but I was smart enough to know I needed to stay in areas of two or three feet of water.

I continued to play in the pool and splash water on other kids. Then I looked over and saw my mom hugging my sister tightly while both were crying and walking frantically back to the hotel room. I had no idea of what was going on.

As I looked around, I overheard someone else say, while pointing to a group of people, *"They…those men and ladies over there…they all jumped in to rescue that little girl from drowning."*

This is the story my sister told me later.

Dianne had sat on the side of the pool and watched the other kids. Some of the ones who could swim started jumping off the diving board. From what she observed, Dianne believed, after the children dove off the board and into the water, they somehow "floated back up to the top." So, she wanted to do the same.

She did not know that they were literally swimming back up from the bottom of the pool. She thought they were just floating up magically. Because she could not swim, Dianne was unaware of the mechanics; she thought she could jump off the board and, just as those kids were doing, "float back up to the top."

No, Dianne, no!!!

So, she proceeded to jump off the diving board into twelve-feet-deep water, not realizing she needed to know how to swim in order to get back to the top. Imagine that. A little Black girl, with long, beautiful, silky black hair extending down her back, approaches the diving board of a pool surrounded only by White people, and it's 1965. Can you imagine what people were saying and thinking? Thank God they were all watching, and it was a good thing a life-guard was on duty as they all watched her dive in.

I remember one lady who also dove in to rescue Dianne. She described to my mom how she intensely watched Dianne as she approached the diving board and surely wondered if Dianne was going to dive in. She kept watching her, and I am sure the lady prepared herself mentally, wondering if she would have to jump in after her.

Thank you, lady!

When after several seconds Dianne did not come back up, about six to eight people dove in—to save my sister's life. When she was rescued, there was no need for mouth-to-mouth resuscitation because Dianne had been down at the bottom of the pool, still holding her breath and trying to figure out how to float back up. Thank God they saved her, got her back up out of the pool, and found my mom.

The next day, everyone at the pool was so nice and kind to us and kept asking us how Dianne was. They made us feel welcome. Several ladies wanted to teach us how to swim. So we took those free lessons, and I learned how to swim. They were nice people, and the people who saved my sister, in my opinion, were not White people; they were good civil people.

They were just like the two nurses who had "yellow hair" in the doctor's office who tended to my burned hand; because some of the ladies at the pool had yellow hair too.

We had a wonderful time at that hotel after Dianne's near-drowning incident. The people vacationing at the motel were not like the folks in Panama City, Florida, and all through the Florida Panhandle, who had signs up that said, "No Negros/Colored People Allowed." If we would had stopped in the panhandle, I really wonder if we would have been harassed? I guess the answer was on those "No Colored People Allowed" signs.

Miami Racism

But all of Miami's population did not stay at our motel, and some people in Miami were not like the people who took a liking to us at the motel.

One night, my mom and her friend let the three of us kids—Dianne, Kate, and me—walk over to the nearest hamburger fast-food joint to get something to eat. It was right across the street from the motel. I can now as an adult conclude the reason they let us go unaccompanied to the fast-food place was probably because everyone at the motel was treating us as equals. There were no racial tensions at the motel; therefore, my mom and Ms. Tatel determined it was okay for us to walk across the street.

We strolled across the street and entered this nice facility to order burgers and fries. Dianne and Kate ordered as I stood around like a dumb seven-year-old little brother. I was observing the red, white, and black decorations. I remember feeling as if we had achieved independence since there was no adult supervision. We waited for the food.

The next thing I remember seeing was the worker forcefully throwing the box of hamburgers and French fries across the counter at Dianne and Kate. This guy literally tossed the box at Dianne and Kate—they almost had to catch it in midair—and said, *"Hea.... y'all food."*

What did we do to get a nice, warm, delicious box of hamburgers and French fries thrown at us? Was it because we were the wrong skin color? I couldn't understand. We had just made friends with several good people at the motel, swimming in the pool, playing and eating hot dogs poolside with them. What was the problem with this kid in the hamburger joint?

I saw the same confusion on Dianne's and Kate's faces as we left. When we arrived back at the motel, Dianne started explaining what happen. My mom asked that we ignore what bad thing just happened and refocus on our vacation. We needed to be the strong, "civilized" ones and ignore other people's feebleness and fears.

That was good advice because, shortly after, we had to return home fast because a hurricane was on its way to

South Florida. Eventually, that same hurricane, Betsy, would destroy New Orleans's Lower Ninth Ward.

Leaving Miami: The Birds and the Bees

We headed home to New Orleans, back to the Desire Housing Project—no white, sandy beach or swimming pool there. Again, I am a seven-year-old ghetto kid and ever so innocent. The vacation to Miami was more than a vacation for me; it was a learning experience. I learned about segregation, experienced an awesome inclusion of integration, saw an act of racism at that hamburger joint, AND, I was about to get my first lesson about the birds and the bees. Though I would soon be lectured on an entirely new social subject, I would not fully comprehend the content until my middle-age years.

During our return trip to New Orleans, we stopped to use the restroom. Dianne, Kate, and I were in the car; my mother and her friend were still using the restroom. While we kids were waiting in the car, Kate and Dianne were playing a rhyming game; I was just sitting there, not participating but listening, and listening intently. One of them would say a word, and the other person would have to rhyme with the next word—such as, cat-hat, mouse-house, and trap-cap. They kept going on and on.

Finally, courageous me, I decided to participate too.

Kate said, "*I ma PRO,*" Dianne said, "*I ma CROW,*" and here comes the ghetto Creole boy who replied, "*I ma HO.*"

Suddenly, it got very quiet in the car. I looked up to see why, and there was this strange look on Dianne's and Kate's faces.

Did I just say something wrong? Why did Dianne and Kate become so quiet after my response? All I said was "I ma ho."

What is a ho anyway? To that day, I had no idea. I don't know why Dianne and Kate decided to rebuke me and then convey to my mother what I said. If they had just left it alone and ignored it, that incident would have passed. Maybe, somewhere during my future life experiences, I would have learned what a ho really was or is. But no! Dianne and Kate had to snitch.

All I said in trying to rhyme and participate in the game was *I am a HO.* All they heard was "the other word." My "ho" was "ho, ho, ho," as in Santa Claus. But no!!! What Dianne and Kate heard in their minds was different.

Dianne told my mom when she returned to the car, and my mom was totally embarrassed. So, on that day, my mom took me to the side and talked to me, trying to explain the meaning of the word Diane and Kate heard.

Did I really need to know the meaning of that word at age seven? Honestly, what and how my mom tried to explain it to me still did not make sense, and I did not fully comprehend her explanation. I will stick to my guns with the word *ho* because on that day all I did was rhyme, HO!! HO!! HO!! as in Merry Christmas.

We continued to drive home, knowing Hurricane Betsy was out over the waters of the Caribbean Sea. We arrived home a couple of days before we knew exactly where Betsy would make landfall. Just a couple of days before, we were in Miami, vacationing and having fun. Then, we were back home, about to be hit by the eye of the storm that would devastate New Orleans, Louisiana.

Hurricane Betsy—Night of Terror

In 2007, I began to write this book; Hurricane Katrina had hit New Orleans two years before. Media and Internet coverage of Hurricane Katrina allowed everyone in the world to see and feel what communities experience during a horrific, catastrophic weather event.

In 1965, Hurricane Betsy hit New Orleans, and it produced as much devastation in the Ninth Ward as Hurricane Katrina did. Katrina, allegedly, broke three levees, all strangely on the east side of three different canals. Whereas for Betsy, the levee or levees in the Ninth Ward were deliberately blown up to preserve the city. Therefore, the Lower Ninth Ward was flooded, on purpose, up to the rooftop of homes in 1965.

We were living in the Desire Housing Project apartments during Hurricane Betsy. My grandmother, Valetta, and my mom's little sister, Melva, were alone in their house on Clouet Street. Gilbert, my step-grandfather, was off at sea, overseas.

Hurricane Betsy came through with 100-plus-miles-per-hour winds in the middle of the night. I was sleeping. I awoke and was instantly frightened by my mother's screaming and hollering—but at or about what? I didn't know. I sat up in bed and I could hear the loud sound of wind as it whipped around outside, and it was very dark in our apartment because the electricity had gone out. There were just a couple of candles burning in the living room.

My mom was crying extremely loudly and screaming out to God, *"Please save ma mama and ma sister; please, God, save ma mama and sister."*

I got up out of bed and walked into the living room; I went over to the window. As I looked out, I saw the wind was blowing mightily, and the trees were moving back and forth. I could see waves of water over the tops of parked cars. Water was everywhere, as far as I could see in the dark. Luckily for us, we were on the second floor of the apartment building. All of the Desire Housing Project buildings and entrance locations were built about six feet high aboveground. Therefore, the floodwater stopped at the top step of each entrance, not entering the hallway on the first floor.

As the wind continued to blow, more water flooded the streets, and my mom was still crying uncontrollably and praying in our candlelit apartment. My sister and I just sat on the couch, not moving.

Then, unexpectedly, in the black of darkness, someone knocked on our front door. *Who would be knocking at our front door during this storm? Maybe it's someone else in one of the other apartments of our complex needing help from us?* Due to the roar of the wind, we had not heard anyone come up the wooden steps.

My mom jumped up and asked who it was. I couldn't hear the person's response, but my mom did. She hurried and opened the door. There stood Valletta and Melva, drenching wet and cold.

My mom really started crying for joy then and thanking Jesus that they were still alive. She was so happy to see her mom and sister and to know they were okay physically. The mental agony and torment they had gone through earlier that night, I would not wish on anyone. My grandmother and aunt Melva's home was taken over by the floodwaters. They only lived about three-quarters of a mile from us in a small wooden house that my grandparents owned in the Ninth Ward on Clouet Street.

When the levees broke earlier that night, or when the authorities exploded the levees, the floodwaters came into the Ninth Ward communities so fast that my grandmother Valetta and aunt Melva, who was only in night grade, found themselves in darkness and standing on top of the bed, with water up to their chests, and still rising.

Imagine this if you can. It is pitch-black, wind blowing loudly, furniture and clothing floating in the house everywhere. All you can see and feel is cold water up to your chest while standing on top of a bed. You hear other people in the neighborhood, next door or across the street, screaming and crying at the top of their lungs for someone to help or rescue them. PURE HORROR.

Many families in the Ninth Ward during Hurricane Betsy had to get up into their attics and break through their roofs to get on top of the house because the water was up to the ceilings in many homes, just as we saw people do on TV during Katrina. Thank God he sent his angels to rescue people, and those angels were local men with boats! They went from house to house, rescuing people. They rescued my relatives and brought them to our apartment that night. May God bless those men; they were courageous and true heroes that night.

To this day, fifty-plus years later, my aunt Melva will not talk about that experience because it was too traumatic for her. I don't think she ever got over it, and my grandmother found religion after that horrific, distressing event. She became a devoted, born-again, holy-roller, Bible-carrying Christian.

Praise the Lord: Too Much Church

My grandmother already had a strong belief in God, but that Hurricane Betsy experience made her take her religious experience and Christianity to another level. She would literally drag us to a different church event or church service or church revival tent meeting every week once our lives returned to normalcy after Betsy.

One time, a big tent-camp revival meeting came to the Desire Housing Project area. There we were, right up on the front row, praising the Lord. I probably got saved about a hundred times between the ages of seven and ten. During those church revivals, every time a preacher offered an altar call, I went up to get saved. I figured that's what the preacher wanted because he kept asking people to come up, so I would go up. My grandmother never stopped me, bless her heart.

One time, we attended a fake church's revival meeting. Even my grandmother was upset, and probably started to doubt her Christianity after that service. It was at the Municipal Auditorium, a civic building presently located in New Orleans's Armstrong Park; it has hosted concerts, graduations, Mardi Gras balls, and sporting events.

It was an Easter weekend. The auditorium was packed, and it seated about four thousand. Before the preacher started preaching and as we—my mom, Dianne, Melva, my grandmother, and me—were entering to find seating, there was a coffin or casket of some kind on the stage. It had been on the stage from the very beginning of the meeting. When the service started and the preacher began preaching, I fell asleep and stayed asleep during the entire sermon.

An hour or two later, I was suddenly awakened by a loud alarm sound. Everyone, including us, started heading for the exits, not knowing if it was a true fire alarm or just a drill similar to those in school. I thought the place was on fire, and the fire alarm had been set off. As we were swiftly walking out, I looked back at the stage while holding on to one of my family member's hands, and there was this middle-aged White lady dressed in all-white linen clothes. She was moving around or dancing across the stage. The preacher was still on the stage, preaching and begging the people to come back.

I remember listening to my grandmother, Melva, and my mom's conversation as we were walking out. They said that the supposedly dead lady that popped out of the casket resembled the preacher's wife. She was dressed in all white and had thick white makeup all over her face and body. From my understanding of the conversation, the preacher was performing a raising-of-the-dead ceremony during that service, and the supposed dead person in the coffin was really his very-much-alive wife. During the ceremony, a loud horn sounded off; it was supposed to represent the trumpet of God blowing and bringing the dead back to life.

Now, I know why everyone ran out of there. In my opinion, if this preacher had the power to raise someone from the dead, then he probably should have had the audience meet him in the city morgue or one of the numerous graveyards in the city. There are a lot of dead people in the graveyards. How about Marie Laveau, New Orleans's famous Voodoo Queen? She was buried in Saint Louis Cemetery No. 1, right across the street from this event. I am sure the Voodoo Queen would have loved to come back to life that night.

I don't remember our attending another large church revival meeting after that one, though we still went to church. About four blocks away from my grandmother's home on Clouet Street, there was a Baptist church on Louisa Street. My grandmother made Dianne, Melva, and me attend a church service with her one night. When we entered the church and looked for seats, Melva and Dianne ran to sit in the very back row of the church, and I decided to sit five or six rows in front of them on the end of the pew, down the middle aisle. My grandmother went and sat up on the front row.

Dianne and Melva were in the back of the church, giggling and playing around like typical young girls. Dianne was around twelve years old, and Melva was about seventeen. I turned around and glared at them; they poked their tongues out at me and started laughing, true sinners playing in church.

The services started with singing and very loud music; I was just sitting and drifting into a daze, daydreaming and looking around. As the music got louder, people started to clap fast and wave their hands and arms; then this lady jumped up and started to dance. The music got even louder, and they were banging drums as the woman continued to dance, jumping up and down and screaming and speaking in tongues. I guess she had or caught what is referred to as the Holy Ghost or the Holy Spirit. I think it had to be the ghost, not the spirit because she was scaring the hell out of me, jumping up and down and moving around uncontrollably.

Eventually, she danced her way to the back of the church, up and down the middle aisle, and then she started coming towards me. I turned around to look at Dianne and Melva; they were trying to either duck or crawl under the pew, thinking the crazy dancing lady wouldn't see them. I wasn't uncomfortable in any church environment or events because of my previous experiences while attending different church services, having been taken by my grandmother from one holy-roller church revival to another, every week. I was accustomed to hearing people speak in tongues and dance in church.

So, this lady in church was dancing towards me. When she positioned herself next to me in the middle aisle, she stopped moving forward but continued to dance in place. While dancing, stomping, and jumping up and down, the lady reached over and grabbed my left arm and lifted it up, trying to get me out of my seat. I just sat there; I did not stand up to dance with her. Finally, I assume she got tired and realized I was not about to get up and dance, no matter how hard she pulled on my arm to lift me out of my seat, or how loud she screamed in other tongues. I guess the lady was praying for me, I am not sure why.

My grandmother just watched the entire time, not saying or doing anything. The two real sinners, whom she should have approached and made dance with her, were Melva and Dianne. They were sitting there in the back of church, laughing, giggling, and acting silly. They, not I, were the ones who needed to get saved and filled with the Spirit that night.

Alabo Street, Lower Ninth Ward, Fats Domino's House

We moved from the Desire Housing Project to the Lower Ninth Ward, Alabo Street, in the spring of 1966. The area we moved to had been totally under water during Hurricane Betsy just months before, but we moved down to the Lower Ninth Ward anyway. All I can figure out is that my parents made a major decision to move out of the Desire Housing Project, even if it meant temporarily moving to the once-flooded Lower Ninth Ward.

We lived not far from Fats Domino's house. My mom would drive pass it often just for us to see where Fats lived. My sister and I would marvel at all of Fats's Cadillacs, his big tour bus, and that nice big, beautiful pink- and white-painted home. In the late fifties and early sixties, to say you lived up the street or in the same neighborhood as Fats Domino was the equivalent of saying you lived up the street from Michael Jackson.

Chapter IV

Back to Creole Village

After about six months in the Lower Ninth Ward on Alabo Street, in the fall of 1966, we moved back to Creole Village, right in the heart of the Seventh Ward, on Annette Street between Tonti and Rocheblave Streets. We were out of the Desire Housing Project and Lower Ninth Ward, but the Ninth Ward mentality was still a part of my sister and me.

While living on Annette Street in the Seventh Ward, my sister and I would encounter social-class differences within the Black community of New Orleans for the first time in our lives.

Home on Annette Street in the Seventh Ward.
Ms. Marie's house was next door to the left.

New Orleans's Black Social-Class Differences

What I am about to write about is exceedingly difficult for me. It is exceptionally uncomfortable for me to write about this subject matter because it is unspoken of in public among Black people in New Orleans. However, it is discussed at kitchen tables in different households and kept within the household. But for you the reader, I must honestly write about this social struggle within the Negro, Black, African American, dark-complexion, light-complexion community; it's vital to the comprehension of this culture of people in New Orleans during the fifties, sixties, and early seventies.

When I was young, I did not thoroughly comprehend the "conflict differences," especially as it relates to the skin-complexion differences within the Black community of New Orleans. Over the years, there has not been enough open verbalization or written communication about the race differences in the Black community of New Orleans, and I cannot say I am an authority on the subject. But I can share with you my personal experiences that will help shed some light on the subject. The topic of dark-complexion/light-complexion continues to be hush-hush or swept under the rug.

The real fact, however, is that there were two classes of Black people in New Orleans during my childhood. There was the African/BlackAmerican class, and there was the Creole/Mulatto/African/Black American class.

As stated early, I am not an expert on this subject, but I will try to share some of my knowledge and discuss those skeletons in the Black community's closet. Those bones are of the two different New Orleans Black communities that I observed as a young kid. The differences in culture and class in the Black community of New Orleans, is no different from what happened in the White communities in the early-late 1900s among the early immigrants of Irish, Italians, and the Jewish communities, and still happens today. In the early New Orleans Black communities,

I know of a few social clubs and organizations and what their memberships usually typified. Without going into detailed research, every New Orleanian who grew up in New Orleans during the thirties, fourties, fifties, sixties, and even seventies, know that membership in a social club was possibly determined by class status and sometimes based on skin complexion.

It has been hush-hush for years that some private social clubs in New Orleans were "brown-paper-bag clubs" dating back before the fifties. Supposedly, to qualify for membership, you had to simply pass the brown-paper-bag test. To pass the test, your skin had to be lighter than the brown paper bag. Honestly, no one placed a brown paper bag against someone's arm or facial skin. "Brown-paper-bag test" was just a term used to describe the light complexion Black clubs. There were some people of a darker complexion in those clubs too, but only a few. On the contrary, in the majority of dark-complexion clubs, there were only a few light-complexion members.

Light complexion Black individuals did not start joining some traditional social clubs until the late sixties and early seventies, when it was becoming trendier to be a member for political connections within the African American community, especially if you were a politician in need of votes.

When it came to attending public or Catholic schools in the forties, fifties, and sixties, light-complexion Creole/Black people made up over eighty percent of Catholic grammar and high school enrollments. You can research and find pictures of students at Xavier University Preparatory High School, Saint Mary's Academy High School, Saint Augustine High School, Epiphany, Corpus Christi, Saint Peter Claver, or

Saint Leo the Great Catholic schools; during the 1970s and before and you will see that many students are of light complexion.

Writing about this is hard for me because there are remnants of these social-class differences still in our community today. I am not writing on this subject in order to prove anything. I am only documenting the class differences that existed in New Orleans when I was growing up as a frame of reference for what I observed as I was growing up.

For me personally, I thought everyone was equal because in my family we loved each other. My family's skin complexions—especially those of my grandparents, uncles, and aunts—went from one extreme to the other. No one kicked me out of my family because I was "high yellow" as referred to by local people in the community. While, socially, I was looked upon as Creole and called "White boy" constantly, there was no treating me differently or special in my family because I was light complexion. Actually, my sister, with her smart brains, received all of the attention.

Epiphany "Creole" Catholic School

Creole Village in the Seventh Ward during 1967 taught my sister and me that there were two Black communities in New Orleans. Living in Creole Village offered my sister and me new challenges or opportunities, and that was to go to school with other Creole children. At first, we did not fit in well or transition easily into this new Creole community at Epiphany Catholic Elementary School. I do not know what it was. Maybe it was the way I smelled or talked or something else, but the boys were mean, mischievous, selfish, arrogant, and crybabies. They always wanted to fight, and fight with me. I had never been around so many spoiled Creole kids in my life up to that point; they wanted to fight all the time over and about any little thing. Back in the Ninth Ward, yes, I got beat up a couple of times because kids thought I was White, but at Saint Philip, we never had fights in school over simple things, or maybe I was just too young to notice. These Seventh Ward Creole kids at Epiphany were not pleasant to be around.

Yes, these little spoiled, high yellow, brats always wanted to fight. Why in the hell did they want to fight with me so much? There was this one kid named Terry. He was an academically challenged Creole kid who had been "held back" in the third grade a couple of times because he could not pass the subjects needed to advance to the next grade. So, Terry really should have been in the fifth or sixth grade, but there he was in third grade with smaller kids; he was a big bully. One day, he tried to start a fight with me, so I did what I would normally do back in the Desire Housing Project. I told my sister. We can conclude that Terry never intimidated me again once Big Dee got ahold of him.

It was told to me, because I never saw the butt kicking firsthand, that it only took one hit; my sister punched Terry in the middle of his back so hard that he could not stand up and walk for about five minutes. He had to sit or lie down for a couple of minutes before his legs would function. After that beatdown, with all the other spoiled Creole kids watching, the word got out not to mess with me because they knew my sister would whip their butts. So, you see, my sister and I did not intermingle well with these spoiled Creole brats at first, and they did not associate well with us either—the transition took some time.

As the school year went on, I started making friends and settling in. Dianne and I started to slowly assimilate into Seventh Ward life. As I started hanging out more with those spoiled Creole brats, I unfortunately picked up on some of their language and bad behavior.

Epiphany Catholic Church, Duels Street,
Seventh Ward, New Orleans, Louisiana.

Epiphany Catholic Gymnasium,
Saint Anthony Street, New Orleans, Louisiana.

Fight of the Decade, Fourth Grade

The fighting and the bullying by those Creole kids carried over into fourth grade. I got into a major clash one day with a Creole Kid in my fourth grade class. I can't remember what caused the clash, but all the kids in our class kept instigating the matter, to the point that we decided to meet on the corner across the street, right after school, to handle our business.

In other words, "Fight after school!"

So, on that day, right at the end of the school day, I and about twenty other kids, along with the kid whom I was going to fight, walked across the street to the corner grocery store, and we started fighting. Across the street from school was off school property, so we were within our legal rights to fight off campus without getting suspended. Smart, right?!

We started our little fight, moving around in a circle, throwing punches, and wrestling on the ground. All I could hear were kids making a lot of noise—screaming, laughing. We just kept moving around in a circle while wrestling.

Then, like a bolt of lightning, I was being snatched up by the neck by our fourth-grade teacher, a nun named Sister Ignacio. She was a White nun about five foot two and chubby. She came across the street to the corner where we were fighting, broke through the crowd, grabbed both of us by the neck, and hauled—and I mean hauled—our little butts back to the school. She firmly grabbed the back of our necks from the back, almost choking us. I was in her right hand, and the other kid was in her left. I was trying keep up with her pace, but she was walking so fast that I kept losing my footing. When I did, my feet would drag on the ground.

I can remember her saying, *"Oh! Y'all wanna fight? Okay, I'll let y'all fight!"*

This nun dragged us back to our fourth-grade classroom; then she picked two girls from the crowd—they were members of our fourth-grade class—and made them push all the chairs in our classroom to one side of the room.

After that, she told us, *"If y'all wanna fight, ya gonna have to do it in front of me."*

I wasn't finished, but I guess she thought I wasn't brave enough to fight in front of her. I can't speak for the other kid, but I was tired of those little snobby, cruel, rotten, arrogant, spoiled-brat Seventh Ward Creole kids picking on me every day. It was time for me to handle my own business without calling on my sister to protect me. It was time for me to stand up and fight my own fight.

So we started fighting again. Yes, in the classroom, and the funny thing is that Sister Ignacio did not watch us fight. I guess she thought now that she'd hauled us back into the classroom, we would not have the nerve to fight on school property, in fear of getting suspended. Sister Ignacio and the two girls started cleaning the chalkboard, emptying the trash, and grading papers while we were fighting. Can you believe that? We had no crowd to watch us, at least not in the classroom, but all those kids that were on the street corner followed us back to the classroom too. They had to stay outside, so they all ran around the building to watch through the windows.

The lower halves of the windows for the entire school were tinted, one could not see out or in, but the upper halves were regular clear glass. If you were tall enough, you could see in or out easily. The crowd outside was enthusiastic and desperate about seeing this fight, and they could not see in through the first level of windows. Therefore, several of the boys went over to the back of the cafeteria, grabbed the big aluminum trash cans, brought those canisters to the fourth-grade classroom windows, and positioned those canisters against the building wall. The students and our classmates could then stand on top of the trash cans to see in through the second level of windows. Some other kids had their bikes and leaned their bikes against the wall, standing on top of the seats and looking into the second level of windows. It was crazy and wild! These kids were cheering as if this were a real championship fight.

Now that I think about it, maybe it was the Fight of the Decade.

Remember, I am from the Ninth Ward, and there was a local saying often used by persons from the Ninth Ward: "I am from the Nine and don't mind dying."

So standing in this corner is the Ninth Ward Ruler, and in the other corner, the Seventh Ward Creole Brat.

Let's...GET READY TO RUMBLE!

The classroom building on side of Epiphany Gymnasium, where the Fight of the Decade took place.

We were fighting inside of the classroom, and I mean going at it for about ten minutes. Believe it or not, the Ninth Ward Ruler was getting the best of the Seventh Ward Spoiled Brat. I had watched my sister fight several times when we lived in the Desire Project, so I guess I had picked up on some of her moves. I was really having a good time punching and beating up on this kid. He could not fight. He became so frustrated at the butt whipping that he started trying to grab me and wrestle. Somehow, he got behind me, wrapped his arms around my neck, and started choking me. Now? Is it dying time for the one from the Nine?

That is when Sister Ignacio stopped the fight and separated us. Then she violently grabbed each of us individually and shook us brutally, to the point that I thought my bodily organs would fall out. She screamed at us about the appalling conduct of fighting, and then she slapped both of us in the face several times. Yes, she allowed us to fight in our fourth-grade classroom; then she stopped the fight, pulled us apart, lectured us about the indecency of fighting, and had the audacity to *slap* us in the face several times before sending us home. Can you believe that? A woman of the cloth slapping nine- or ten-year-old boys in the face?

My mom wasn't happy about the marks on my face from the slapping, and when I described to her all the details of the fight, my mom made a visit to Sister Ignacio. You'll have to ask my mom for the rest of that story. That is her story; the fight story is mine.

Altar Boy at Epiphany

While attending Epiphany, I got into a couple more fights, none as dramatic as the Fight of the Decade. I also became an altar boy. All the older Creole altar boys were bullies, all of them, and those Creole bullies got the first pick of the church's services, masses, weddings, and funeral services. Because I was a new altar boy, I always got stuck with doing the worst church service of all—the weekday 6:00 a.m. church mass or a Saturday morning funeral. No other altar boys wanted to do funerals on Saturday mornings because Saturday mornings were for watching cartoons on TV and playing outside, but I had to do funeral services on Saturdays several times. The reason the older altar boys preferred weekday funerals was because, if those occurred during school hours, they had an acceptable excuse for missing school that morning or possibly all day.

One time, I lucked out and got scheduled to do a funeral during the week. Usually, three to four altar boys helped during a funeral service. At the end of this funeral service, the priest said he would only need two of us to go to the graveyard site to help with the burial of the body. As was typical, I got bullied out of going by two of those Creole kids, so I had to stay behind and go to school.

But I started thinking—instead of going to class, I was going to make the best of that day until they got back. So, I hid out in a closet in the back of the church until they returned from the graveyard site, and we all went back to class together. I earned some spoiled-brat brownie points that day because those two Creole kids thought that was cool of me to hide out until they got back. They had never done that before, and they started telling the other altar boys what I did. From there, they all planned to do the same in the future when they were not scheduled to attend the grave site during a school-day-scheduled funeral.

The Wedding—Social-Class Division

I never assisted as an altar boy for a wedding because weddings were special if you were an altar boy; you got paid usually five or ten dollars by the wedding party to assist the priest with the wedding service. All the older Creole altar boys monopolized the weddings, even if they occurred on Saturday morning. Sometimes, the older Creole altar boys would fight over who was going to assist with the next wedding on the schedule because they knew money was involved. Again, I never got scheduled for weddings, not one, but one day I was told I had to do a wedding. I was ecstatic.

The wedding was set for the coming Saturday afternoon. That was fine with me, and it did not matter that I did not know who was getting married. All I concentrated on was getting paid five or ten dollars. My first wedding. I went home, told my mom I had a wedding to do, so she helped me get my clothes ready for that Saturday morning.

Saturday came around, and off to the wedding I went. I don't even think my mom worried or inquired about who was getting married either. It did not matter. There was a wedding, a couple needed an altar boy, and I was available. But still I could not believe that I was summoned to assist with a wedding.

The bride was an unbelievably beautiful, light complexion Creole lady, and the male was a dark complexion , handsome gentleman. It did not matter to me; I didn't see skin complexions. All I saw were two people in love, wanting to get married. Why would a nine- or ten-year-old kid be concerned with skin complexion?

Years later, I know why I was asked to assist in this wedding by the priest that week. Either none of the other altar boys wanted to do it, or they were not permitted to by their parents. I am only speculating here, but I genuinely believe gossip about whom this beautiful Creole lady was marrying went out throughout the Creole community around Epiphany Church. Those parents told their sons who were altar boys not to accept the invite to assist in the wedding. This is just my personal belief, but I know how stubborn some older Creole people can be. If they did not like a situation or did not agree with what was happening, or if someone acted contrary to what they believed were the Creole culture's traditional values, you were an outcast.

Usually, two altar boys are asked to assist with a wedding, but for this wedding, I was the only one. There I was, innocent me, standing at the front of the church and watching this beautiful light-complexion bride come down the aisle. The bride was to my right; therefore, all her family members and friends were sitting on her left side. All of them were light complexion —all. The groom was on my left side; therefore, all his family members were sitting on his right side. All of them were of a dark- complexion —all. As I am standing there on the alter stage in the front of the church, looking at the congregation of people that are attending this wedding, I see "Black" people, sitting in Church, divided by skin complexion, unbelievable.

As the wedding started, I looked up at the groom, and he was a handsome gentleman. He looked back at me and gave me a wink of his eye, as if saying, *"Hey there, little fella, thank you for being courageous enough to assist with our wedding. You made this work for us."*

The wedding proceeded, and no one—THANK GOD, no one—objected to these two beautiful people getting married. So, they jumped the broom.

As time passed, I would see this couple in the community now and then, sometimes at the supermarket or at a high school football game. Every time they saw me, they would say, *"Hey, there is our altar boy."* I would politely speak or wave.

Annette Street—Are We Sure We're Negro?

Down on the corner from our house on Annette Street in the Seventh Ward were two -light complexion Creole brothers, Alvin and Allen. Alvin was the younger, and he was closer to my age. Allen was about three years older. These guys, they looked White, but they were remarkably pale- complexion Creoles. There complexion was so fair that people knew I was Black when I stood next to them.

One day, in either 1966 or 1967, the three of us rode our bicycles over to the New Orleans Fire Station on St Philip Street, one block off Broad Street, to register our bikes. We had to ride through a White neighborhood on Dorgenois Street, between Saint Bernard and Orleans Avenues. When we arrived at the fire station on the corner of Saint Philip and Dorgenois Streets, we got off our bikes and walked inside to register them. We wanted those nice little bike license plates that made your bike look cool.

As we walked in, I noticed a White fireman and policeman, and they were staring at us. They just kept looking at us as if something were wrong. One of them finally got enough courage to ask what our race was, and we told him, "Negro."He could not believe it. He asked us again, *"Are ya'll sure you are Negroes?"*

We said, Yep....!

The fireman and policeman began to laugh, and that was the end of that conversation. We got on our bikes with those nice little license plates hanging on the back of our bikes, and we headed back home.

Why were they laughing? I don't know. Maybe it was their way of belittling people who were multiracial.

Civil Rights Movement—Black Power

Around 1966-68 was the height of the Civil Rights Movement. On April 4, 1968, I noticed my mother was glued to the TV. She was just sitting there in front of the TV, staring into that small black and white screen. I remember this as if it were yesterday.

As I looked over to the TV, the news anchor was describing the assassination of Dr. Martin Luther King Jr. I can't say as a ten-year-old that I knew the entire political/social scene at that time or had a full understanding of it. All I know is, that day, I learned who Dr. Martin Luther King Jr. was and what an impact he had on our society. I continued to watch the TV news anchor and the story of the killing of Dr. King. The news coverage switched to riots and violence in several major cities across the country. I remember watching and seeing people looting and cars and buildings on fire.

I remember one story out of Detroit. A man was just trying to go home after work to get his family out of the neighborhood and take them to a safer environment. The police started shooting at his car and killed the poor man—right there on the TV. My world outlook transformed; I realized that this wasn't the innocent world I had perceived it to be. After watching all the violence that was taking place in other cities, my mom got a piece of black cloth, tore it into a long, narrow strip, wrapped it around my arm, and told me to wear it around my arm for the next several days. That black piece of material wrapped around my arm was a sign to Black militants that I was Black and believed in "Black Power."

I had no idea what the Black Power movement was, but I started believing in Black power that day. Based on what we were seeing and hearing on the news about what was happening in other cities, my mom did not want some confused person to think I was White. Though New Orleans escaped some of the major rioting problems other cities had, my mom did not want anyone to hurt me.

The only problem we had in our neighborhood during this tumultuous period that I know of was at the corner store, Miller Grocery Store. A White family owned it; they were very nice people who respected others and never did harm to anyone. I remember Mr. Miller. He was a genuinely nice, tall gentleman with a slightly bald head; he wore glasses. He was always nice to me and to everyone.

Someone or some group tried to burn down their corner store, but luckily only the front outside of the building got slightly burned. The firemen arrived in time to put the fire out before it caused major damage.

Miller Grocery Store on Annette Street.

On one of my visits to the store after the fire, Mr. Miller was talking to someone. He had a very confused expression on his face when he said, *"I can't understand who or why someone would do this to us?"*

I looked up at him and thought to myself, *Me too, Mr. Miller. Why?*

Chapter V

Sixth and Seventh Wards—People and Places

Fun Times

Ms. Marie (Pronounced MAW-REE)

We made it through those turbulent times of the middle '60s. The Seventh Ward was a very ideal working-class community, and we all know every community has unique characters. One of those individuals lived next door to us.

Ms. Marie, our neighbor, was an exceptionally beautiful, older Creole/Native American character who lived next door to us on Annette Street. We did not pronounce Ms. Marie's name "Ma-ree"; it was pronounced "Maw-ree." Ms. Marie lived next door in her fourplex home, a picture of which is at the beginning of chapter four. Standing in front of her home and looking at it, she lived up on the second floor, on the right side of that fourplex.

A fourplex house has two apartments at the top and two at the bottom. There are stairs in the middle. Ms. Marie lived directly next door to us on the second level. If she stood at her front door and looked to her left, there would only be about twelve feet of distance between our front door and hers.

Ms. Marie was a retired "lady of the night." She had to be around seventy or seventy-five years old. She had long, beautiful, silky black hair like a Native American's. Her skin complexion was also an amazingly beautiful olive tone, and she was very skinny. She was probably a mix of Indian, Black, and White. She had tattoos on both of her upper shoulders.

I remember my mom telling us that Ms. Marie was probably an attractive lady back in her "days of grandeur." But for me, Ms. Marie was just this old lady with long black hair who sat out on the porch every day. As I entered or exited our apartment, she would speak and wave, and I would do the same in return. We respected her as a neighbor, and my mom would speak with her occasionally in general conversations about the weather or simple social issues.

Ms. Marie was a quiet person who just sat out on the porch every day and watched everything that went on in the neighborhood. No one would go up her stairs to speak with her, nor would she come down those stairs to speak with anyone. I only saw Ms. Marie off her porch once or twice.

One day she was walking to Millers Grocery Store early in the morning. She wore a very tight red skirt and a black blouse. I watched her as she walked with her long black hair and those skinny legs. I kept staring at her because I'd never seen her walk before, other than in and out of her front door to sit in her chair on her porch or to go back inside her apartment. I never saw her hold a conversation with anyone. She just very quietly sat outside in her chair on the porch. In other words, as New Orleanians would say, "She minded her own business."

But other people in the neighborhood did not mind their own business when it came to Ms. Marie. I would hear other kids say weird and strange things about her, and those kids probably heard those rumors from their parents. Therefore, I did not know if those rumors were true. People said she practiced voodoo and had dead people's bones in one of the bottom apartments. They also said that men would visit her late at night, and into the early morning hours.

I never saw men go in or out of her house. I do remember Ms. Marie having a husband, but he was always in the house. Maybe those men were creeping in and out of Ms. Marie's house during the early, dark mornings when most people should be sleeping instead of poking their noses in other people's business. Since I never saw men go in and out of Ms. Marie's home, maybe those kids' parents were referring to events that happened in Ms. Marie's house some twenty or thirty years earlier. The Seventh Ward was known for people just standing with the front door open or looking out of their windows day and night to see, hear, or observe what other people were doing—in other words, being nosy.

Another rumor was that Ms. Marie's house had a bad odor or stank. I knew that was not true because we lived right next door to her; I don't ever remember a bad smell coming out of her front door or windows. One thing I do know—the only odor I would smell from her house was that of cooked food, and it sure smelled good. So, I have no idea why those kids in the neighborhood would say such awful things and spread such terrible rumors about this lady. Also, how could they presume her house smelled bad when no one had ever been in her house?

Ms. Marie had one of the biggest Japanese plum trees in her backyard; she also had two big dogs. My two Creole friends who lived at the corner, Alvin and Allen, were two of the rumor kids; they would stand along my backyard fence and gaze into hers, trying to come up with a plan as to how we were going to get those plums off the tree without her dogs attacking us.

One day, the dogs were in the house, and we had our one chance. We quickly jumped the fence and started ripping the plums off that tree as if we were madmen. We were trying to hurry because we did not want Ms. Marie to let the dogs out on us. Well, the dogs never came out, and I never heard those dogs bark in the house. I think that day she allowed us to get those plums off the tree, so she kept the dogs in the house. We ripped off a ton of plums that day and ate them all.

Alvin—my friend who was so thrilled to steal plums off the tree and was the primary rumor schmoozer—initiated a major confrontation with Ms. Marie one day. For some strange reason, this kid went up the stairs while Ms. Marie was sitting on her porch. He told her some things he'd heard his mother repeat to other people about Ms. Marie and her home—Seventh Ward gossip, he said/she said stuff.

I was in my house, probably watching cartoons on TV, and I started hearing people outside screaming at each other. I walked outside and saw Alvin's mother standing in front of Ms. Marie's house with Alvin. Ms. Marie was off her porch, standing on her steps and yelling at Alvin's mother.

I later found out what happened earlier that day to cause this major confrontation. Alvin walked up the steps to visit with Ms. Marie and reported to her a conversation of his mother's that he'd overheard. Alvin's mother told someone that Ms. Marie's house had an odor and that the two empty apartments below had dead people's bones in them. I remember Alvin's mother swearing loudly and hysterically, trying to persuade Ms. Marie that she did not say those awful things about her. The next thing that happened was strange and funny.

Right at the time Ms. Marie had started believing his mother, Alvin looked up and screamed, *"You did say those things, Mom. Stop lying; you did say those things."* That was not very smart of him. I don't know what got into him that day to go and inform Ms. Marie that his mother was gossiping about her.

About that time, several neighbors are either standing in their doorway or out on their porches, watching and listening to this confrontation. Alvin's mother looked at him and responded very loudly, *"No, I did not say those things."* She then slapped him on the head awfully hard several times.

Ms. Marie, who never meddled in anyone's business, was not about to take this belittlement sitting down; she was undeniably ready to defend herself. That old lady stood there on those steps like a pro fighter, used every rotten-mannered word from A to Z to convey her real feelings towards Alvin's mom, and expressed vehemently to Alvin's mom where to go, where to stick it, what to kiss, and whom to sleep with.

I was proud of Ms. Marie that day; she stood her ground. On top of that, Ms. Marie helped me to increase my filthy vocabulary that day. I did not know you could use such filthy, nasty, dirty words in a complete "creative" sentence the way she did. I would had loved to have seen Ms. Marie fight sixty or seventy years earlier. Even that day, I would have placed all my money on Ms. Marie if it had turned into a physical fight.

That skirmish was the second time I saw Ms. Marie off her porch. Over the next couple of days, things settled back to normal, and I heard that Alvin's mother later revisited Ms. Marie to apologize.

Several weeks after that event, my mom came to me and asked me to go to Ms. Marie's and pick up something she had cooked for us. Why didn't my mom just go and get it herself? Why did she have to send me into that lady's house? If those rumors about dead people's bones in her bottom apartments were true, I could end up in her cooking pot as a good meal. I am scared out of my pants. I do not want to go in that lady's house. I am TERRIFIED.

By accepting what Ms. Marie had cooked for us that day, maybe my mom was trying to make Ms. Marie feel more respected as a good neighbor after that major confrontation with Alvin's mom. Therefore, I followed my mom's instructions, and, like a good Catholic boy, I walked over to Ms. Marie's home to get what she had cooked for us. Whatever it was, I was NOT going to eat it. I dared not. Maybe I should give it to Alvin's mom and let them eat it first, then see what happened.

I slowly approached Ms. Marie's stairs and started walking up them slowly, not wanting to go in her apartment. I then stopped, turned around, went back down the stairs, and sat down on the very bottom step for a while before I got the nerve to go back up.

Ms. Marie came out of her house and yelled over to our apartment, asking where I was. Because our homes were so close together, it was easy to hear someone next door shouting. My mom came to our front door and said she'd sent me over; when she looked down, she saw me sitting on the bottom step. My mom screamed at me to get up and go get the food.

So, I got up and walked up the stairs slowly. Ms. Marie waited for me to get up to the top, where I thought she was going to hand me the food at the door. But she did not. She asked how I was doing; I said okay. She opened the screen door and told me to come in, and with fear in every bone of my body, I entered her home, knowing that this may be the last day of my life. *Why did my mom sentence me to my death at such an early age?*

As I entered the home, something was smelling good, but the scent faded into the background as I looked around and was astonished by what I saw. Based on all the rumors and erroneous information I had heard about this lady and the filth she lived in, I did not expect to find the house IMMAC-ULATE!!!! Not a spot of dirt anywhere.

Either she had cleaned it up that day, or it just stayed clean and neat all the time because she had no kids. I do not know what her motive was for inviting someone into her home. Maybe it was to quiet the neighborhood gossip or to prove to those people that she was not a dirty person. She knew that once I told one person how neat and clean her house was, trust me, through the grapevine, the entire neighbor-hood would know.

On the wall and on top of the mantel, she had these nice old pictures of herself when she was young. Yes, she was a very, very pretty, young lady; I would have dated her. As I looked at the pictures, then looked back at her, she smiled because she knew I was admiring how pretty she was when she was young. She then asked that I follow her into the kitchen to get whatever it was that she cooked for us.

I had no idea of what she'd cooked, but all I could envi-sion was a skeleton head wrapped in aluminum foil on a plate, or something like that. As I got closer to the kitchen, it started to smell extremely good, a sweet smell. Maybe she had put some butter and sugar on a skeleton head and baked the skeleton head.

I entered the kitchen, and there it was—the plate of goodies she'd cooked for us. My eyes opened big and wide because she did not cook a regular plate of food; rather, this nice old lady made us some large pecan pralines, a full plate of them.

For those of you who don't know what pralines are, you take sugar, cream, butter, and pecans, cook them in a pot, pour the mixture in small circles onto a cookie sheet, and then set it out to cool at room temperature or in the refrigerator.

Those pralines were stacked high on a plate; she covered them with some wax paper and gave them to me to take home. She asked me if I liked pralines, and my answer was unconditionally *"YES, MAAEEEM! Thank you very much."*

No way Alvin and his mom were going to taste test them first. If there was poison in those pralines, then I was about to die. "Coming to meet you, Elizabeth," as Fred Sanford would say. And after I die from eating these pralines, you can place my body/bones down in the apartment below with the rest of the people Ms. Marie killed.

I took that plate of pralines home, and we literally killed the entire plate of them.

Clark Bulldogs

If Ms. Marie had shared her pralines with the Joseph S. Clark High School football team, maybe they would have had a chance to win a football game against St. Aug. In the village, there was a killing that took place on the football field. The renowned, all-Black boys' school that I described in an earlier chapter, Saint Augustine Catholic High (Saint Aug), basically killed every public school in football. But on one Sunday afternoon, Joseph S. Clark High School DESTROYED the Saint Aug musical talent show.

One nice spring Sunday afternoon, Saint Aug was conducting a talent show, and it was being held in Corpus Christi Catholic Elementary School's gym, in the spring of '69. I need to make something truly clear—this was Saint Aug's talent show, and it was open to the public for anyone to perform. Most of the crowd attending the talent show were not—repeat, not—from Saint Aug. Instead, it was a Joseph S. Clark High School crowd.

Before 1947, there was only one public high school for Black students in the Sixth and Seventh Wards of New Orleans; that was McDonogh 35. The only other public schools for Black students during that time were mid- and uptown, and those were Booker T. Washington and Walter L. Cohn High Schools.

Clark became another public school in 1947 for Black students in the downtown area until 1958, and that is when George Washington Carver opened in the Ninth Ward. Therefore, Clark High School was the popular public school in the city for both Seventh and Sixth Ward students; it is located on Bayou Road and North Derbigny Street in the heart of the Tremé community.

On a night back in the spring of 1969, the Clark students took over the talent show from the Saint Aug students in the Corpus Christi gym. Because of the domineering Clark students, that event had such an impact on me that I have never forgotten it. The Saint Aug talent show was open to all high school students in the Black community. Therefore, students from other schools could audition and perform, but Clark students were the majority of the crowd that night. Every time one of their school members performed onstage, all you could hear at the end of the performance was the school's name being chanted very loudly and a dog-barking chant.

"CLARK BULLDOGS—WOOF! WOOF! WOOF!"

"CLARK BULLDOGS—WOOF! WOOF! WOOF!"

"CLARK BULLDOGS—WOOF! WOOF! WOOF!"

Joseph S. Clark High School, located on
North Derbigny Street, New Orleans, Louisiana.

Corpus Christi Catholic School and Gym.
Site of Saint Augustine's talent show, 1969.

Corpus Christi Catholic Church, Saint Bernard Avenue, New Orleans, Louisiana.

The village was on fire and wild that night. It was exciting, and everyone was having a good time, screaming and yelling as their favorite person or band performed onstage. There were numerous acts, both groups and solo performers, singing the now-old Motown and other rhythm-and-blues classics.

My aunt Melva performed in this talent show; her song selection was Aretha Franklin's, "I Never Loved a Man (the Way I Love You)."

Aunt Melva and I are sitting on the
porch of her home, 2915 Clouet Street, 1969.

Though she did not win, nor was she honored with any awards that night because the Clark crowd had their favorites, she sang the hell out of the song, just like Aretha.

Saint Augustine Football: King Solomon

The Clark High School students may have taken over Saint Aug's talent show, but one area in which Clark High School could not dominate Saint Aug was in high school football, and especially not the halftime band performance.

If you lived in New Orleans as a high school student in the late sixties and did not attend a Saint Aug football game or a Black public-school game, then you missed one of the best experiences you could have had as a Black youth, because the halftime shows were actually the events, not the games. It really did not matter if your school won the football game. Just dare not squander the halftime show.

There was this one player on the Saint Aug football team, from 1966 through 1969, who went by the nickname King Solomon, and he wore number forty-four. He was one of the most electrifying football players to ever play at Saint Aug, though he did not go on to have a major pro career. During any Saint Aug game, when it was time for King Solomon to receive the kickoff or punt return, all the fans would stand up in anticipation that he would return it for a touchdown. I promise you; he was a superior high school athlete. I am giving this guy props here, and I don't know him personally, nor did I ever have a chance to meet him.

The Saint Aug marching band was the best in the land, and the halftime shows without question were the biggest events at the games.

In the seventies, when Saint Aug entered the all-White Class "4-A", high school conference,Saint Aug could not win a game in those beginning years. I am not going to try and provide problematical reasons why, although it did seem as if Saint Aug should have won some games that they lost when playing in this new classification, because numerous penalty flags against them were inevitable. The "4-A" conference/classification was often referred to as the Catholic League, but that was far from the truth because Chalmette High School was a public school, and yes the only public school in this classification.

Without question, halftime was another story. Halftime belonged to the "brothers" and the Marching 100. They would perform plenty of the R&B hits that we heard on the radio, and, yes, there was plenty of dancing in the City Park Stadium seating area.

Dear Friends: The Wilsons

One of my sister's closest friends lived in the village on Annette Street, up the street from us, and her name was Pam. Her family were some of the nicest people you would ever meet in your life. This family was not the traditional Seventh Ward, light complexion Creole family and we were very to close with this family, often at their home and they at our home. Pam's dad was a construction worker, but to earn some extra money, he and his older sons repaired cars. This man, Mr. Wilson, was so nice to my family; he would repair our cars every time they needed fixing. My mom would try to pay him, but he would argue and not take the money. He took money from other people once he repaired their vehicles, but he felt as if we were family. My mom would just place down the money somewhere and then leave; I am sure he would eventually see it, pick it up to give to his wife.

Pam's two older brothers attended Clark High School. One of her brothers was in Clark's marching band, and I remember him telling me and his little brothers one day, *"Y'all dink Saint Aug band is good, uh ? Dey not!!. Y'all need da see Clark Bulldog Band. Y'all come to a Clark football game to see a real band."*

So, one Friday fall night, I decided to go to a Clark High School football game with the Wilsons. The game was being held at City Park's Ted Gormley Stadium. Clark was playing against Walter L. Cohen High School from uptown, somewhat of a crosstown rivalry; Cohen had an excellent marching band too. Every time Clark's band struck up a song while the game was being played, Cohen's band would retaliate with a song of their own. So, my attention was fixed on the two bands all night; forget the football game.

The competition between the bands, playing songs back and forth, went on all night. Then at halftime, which was a good show to see, each school tried to outperform the other. The only thing about the football game I remember between those two schools was during a time-out down on the field; a player from Cohen High School was on the field, dancing to a song being played by the Clark band—ironic.

After attending that game, I did not want to tell Pam's older brother that the Clark band, in my opinion, was not as good as Saint Aug's Marching 100. Sorry, Clark, the Bulldogs Band was good, incredibly good, but not as good as the Marching 100.

"CLARK BULLDOGS—WOOF, WOOF, WOOF!!!!!"

The Circle Theater

High school football games on the weekends during fall were good events to attend, but Sunday afternoons were only reserved for one thing, and that was the local movie theater. Many days, especially on those warm summer afternoons, I will never forget how my sister and I would stand in a long line waiting to get into the Circle Theater. If you wanted to catch a King Kong or Godzilla movie, the Beatles or any of the silly sixties movies, the Circle Theater on Sunday afternoons was the place to be.

We would get there to line up around noon or 1:00 p.m. to catch the first showing, and the people waiting would stretch around the corner. Many teenagers from every neighborhood in the village would just hang out and have a good time while waiting for the doors to open. Once inside the theater, it was lights, camera, and action!

More like kissing action, I should say. I watched this one couple kiss during an entire movie one time. I think that is where I learned how to kiss, just by watching that couple.

One movie I remember at the Circle Theater was *Vanishing Point*. It starred Cleavon Little as a blind radio deejay. Throughout most of the movie, he gives advice over the radio to a guy trying to evade the police by driving a fast car through the desert.

The Circle Theater was located on the corner of Saint Bernard Avenue and Galvez Street, across from Corpus Christi, New Orleans, Louisiana.

In several scenes of this movie, policemen are setting up roadblocks in an attempt to catch this guy. There is another scene in which a fully nude White girl shows up on a motorbike.

This is the late sixties, and the viewing audience is all Black kids. When we saw the naked White girl riding that motorbike, we were shocked. Then she got off that motorbike and started walking, fully nude, towards the guy who was driving the speeding car. The place erupted with a very loud "*OOOOOOOO!!!!!*" I was shocked too; it was my first time seeing nudity and pubic hair below the navel on any women, and on top of that, it was on a theater screen.

After watching the couple touching and kissing in the theater, seeing a nude White woman on a movie theater screen, and my introduction to vulgar language from A to Z, thanks to Ms. Marie, my growing up in the village was just beginning.

Christmas in the Village

Speaking of fully nude and nothing on, you dared not let your house go undecorated during Christmas, at least not on our street. The houses on Annette Street, from Galvez Street to Hope Street, would be all decked out for the holiday. Everyone in our area really got into the Christmas spirit and tried to outperform each other when decorating their homes. During Christmas, Annette Street was the place for Black people to see Christmas decorations, and many cars would ride up and down our street all night to view the Christmas display. It was awesome to see.

Mardi Gras in the Village

The village and the street we lived on, Annette, was near the Central Business District of New Orleans, which means during Mardi Gras season, which is usually cold weather, we could walk to Rampart Street and watch all the parades as they turned into the Municipal Auditorium. It was wonderful to walk in the cold weather to and from the parades, it was as if we knew everyone, and everyone knew us. We would see all our friends from the other neighborhoods and kids we went to school with, who were walking to the parade too.

As we walked, we would pass and speak to older people who were sitting out on their porches or on the steps. We always said "good night" or "good evening" because the village was a small community, and, again, many people knew each other. Some of those older people sitting out on their steps or porches knew our parents. We needed to be on our best behavior. If not, when we got home after the parade, our moms would already know what we'd done wrong.

Pontchartrain Beach Amusement Park and Integration

During Christmas, it was traditional for us to stay out late, sit on the steps in the cold, and watch all the cars drive down the street to see all the decorations. During Mardi Gras, we'd be out late too, again in the cold, walking back home from the parades. However, in the summertime, there were other reasons to stay out late and sit on those steps.

The height of the fourplex house in which we lived on Annette Street allowed us the opportunity to stand on the porch, which was on the second level, and look towards the north during summer nights. That's how we would watch the fireworks at Pontchartrain Beach Amusement Park—or just "the Beach," as we would call it—during their nightly closing event.

Although the Civil Rights Act of 1964 was the law by then, Black people did not feel comfortable going to Pontchartrain Beach Amusement Park, which was for Whites only prior to 1964. So, the next best thing was for us was to stand on the second-floor porch and watch the fireworks at the Beach from afar.

In the village we had all the necessities for a family to survive—grocery stores, movie theater, schools, parks, pharmacies, clothing stores, shoe stores, restaurants, etc. Black people knew, however, that we were still not welcome in certain places throughout the city, even though the Civil Rights Act of 1964 had been passed.

One early fall night before the Beach closed for the season, either in 1967 or 1968, my brave mom decided to take me and my sister to Pontchartrain Beach. My mom wanted us to have all that life had to offer, and she decided that was the night Pontchartrain Beach was going to be integrated. We were going to be the integrators.

I am not saying my family was the first to integrate Pontchartrain Beach. I am not sure, maybe we were, but all I know was that on that night, because the Civil Rights Act of 1964 banned public discrimination, my mother decided Pontchartrain Beach was going to be integrated by us. Something just stirred up in my mom, and she said, *"Get ready; we are going to Pontchartrain Beach tonight."*

When we arrived at the park that chilly fall evening, yes, we were the only Black folks in the park. Things went surprising well as we walked around and rode the different rides; we had no racial confrontations. We enjoyed several amusement rides, walked through the mirror maze, and snacked on hot dogs, hamburgers, and popcorn. It was a delightful family outing.

But there is one lifelong image that has stuck with me from our visit to the Beach that night. While standing in line with numerous other people waiting to get on one of the rides, there was this terrible odor in the air. I could not for the life of me figure out where this terrible odor was coming from. In front of us were several teenage girls who were giggling and having a good time. It was a cool spring night, and the wind was blowing slightly, carrying that awful odor to my nose as I stood there. I kept asking my mom and my sister, *"Do y'all smell dat? Wha is dat bad smell?"* My mom told me to keep quiet.

I am only about three and a half feet tall at that point, and everyone around me was taller; therefore, the odor in front of me had to be about three feet high. There were several very tall teenage girls in front of me, and there was a large crowd of teenagers behind us. As we are standing there waiting for the line to move, I am bearing the bad odor.

For some strange reason, the crowd behind us started pushing the line forward. We tried not to move as we stood close together, attempting to stand our ground in one spot and not move forward, but the force and the momentum of the crowd was too strong. The next thing I knew, my face got pushed right into the long brown hair hanging down the back of this teenage girl in front of me.

Guess what? That is where that bad odor was coming from. I had never smelled something so horrible in my life. She probably had not washed her hair, body, or clothes for several days. Nonetheless, it was a very distressing odor for a nine- or ten-year-old kid to smell.

I turned around and told my mom and Dianne about the odor, and once again they told me to be quiet. Okay, I kept quiet.

Eventually we got on the ride that went around and around. No one was quiet then.

Integrating A&G Cafeteria on Canal Street

On another occasion while still living in the village, my mom decided that we were going to be the integrators of another public place. She got this great idea that we should go out to eat. Well, that was a good idea; we often ate at Chez Helene or Lavata's.

But the location my mom decided we would eat that afternoon was not the best place to go, well, not yet anyway. She concluded once again, since the Civil Rights Act of 1964 was passed by Congress and integration was mandated by law, we should go and eat at the A&G Cafeteria/Restaurant on the corner of Broad Avenue and Canal Street.

It did not bother me; all I knew was that we were going to eat at the nice A&G Cafeteria on Canal Street. If we were going to have to stand and wait in a line, this time I wanted to be behind my sister or mom; I did not want another bad-odor experience.

We entered the restaurant, and we had to stand in line with the other folks waiting to get a seat. We were the only Black people in line that day. My mom tells this story better than I do. She says we were the very first Black family to eat at A&G. She confirmed that with the Black cooks in the kitchen that day who kept coming out from the back to look at us. They told her that was why they kept coming out from the kitchen at the back of restaurant—to see if Black people were really in line.

I remember a middle-aged, blonde-headed (not yellow-haired) lady with blue eyes staring at me while we stood in line. Every time I turned around, she was gazing at me with this mean look in her eyes. It made me feel awkward, and I asked my mom why the lady kept staring down at me that way.

My mom's response was the same as it was that night at the Beach—*"Be quiet."*

I guess the lady could not figure out why a little, light complexion , almost-White-looking kid was with two beautiful Black people there in the restaurant. The good news is that the lady staring at me with that mean look was the only significant "immoral" thing that happened that day. We proceeded to walk the line, get our food, sit at a table, and eat the DELICIOUS fried chicken cooked by Black people.

In my opinion, that blonde-haired lady could STARE until she dropped dead. Her stare was not going to stop me from eating that delicious fried chicken. If something dreadful was going to happen, then that fried chicken would be my motivation to stand up for my civil rights. Power to the chicken!!!

Chapter VI

Poplarville, Mississippi

"Hot Fun in the Summertime"—Sly and the Family Stone

As I stated in my dedication, my now-adult children, Herman Jr. and Mary-Naomi, have told me for years, *"Dad, write a book! We are tired of hearing those stories. Please stop telling them."*

Again, thanks, kids!

The reason for their outbursts is that I have overwhelmed them with stories from my past. Most of the stories were about experiences during my summer vacations in Poplarville, Mississippi. I could literally write a book about those experiences alone.

What I learned in Poplarville during those hot summer days helped me to be a grateful person in my adolescent and early adult years and to this day. Those experiences alone undoubtedly kept me focused on life's challenges and how everyone—Black, White, or any other race or nationality—must work hard to be successful in life.

My purpose for sharing a couple of experiences from my years of summer stints in Poplarville is because these experiences helped with my overall social and professional development. These experiences involved social education, valor, bravery, courage, respect, and, of course, sexual consciousness. Besides swimming in ponds and creeks, there were many experiences in which hard work was critical. Gathering watermelons, planting cotton, picking tomatoes, cucumbers, and corn, feeding the hogs, collecting eggs out of the chicken coop, slaughtering live chickens and hogs, then cooking them on a large burner in the backyard. In addition to hard work, which mainly occurred in the hot summertime in the sun, I had many social and religious experiences too.

Josephine and Johnny

How did I end up spending several summers in Poplarville? All I know is that there were these two individuals, Josephine and Johnny were their names, and supposedly we were distant relatives. How and through what lineage, I have no idea.

They lived in another area of the Desire Housing Project, which is where we lived during the early sixties, until 1966. They literally lived across the street from the local New Orleans chapter of the Black Panthers, they were Jehovah's Witnesses, and they had five children around the age of my sister and me.

Johnny's side of his family was from Poplarville, Mississippi. He moved from Poplarville to New Orleans in search of employment during the late fifties and found work down at the riverfront unloading ships and working different construction sites in the meantime. Johnny would visit Poplarville almost every weekend because he was a country boy, and he loved going home to visit.

My mom sometimes needed an additional babysitter when Valetta or Aunt Thelma were not available, so we would stay at Josephine and Johnny's place. I know I cannot speak for my sister, but sometimes I hated going there. They never had enough food, and the apartment was always dirty and smelly. I think I even got bitten on the arm by a rat or spider while sleeping one night.

But fact is fact; we just managed and made do with that situation. Don't get me wrong, what I did like about going there was getting the opportunity to play and socialize with Johnny and Josephine's children. We were in the same age bracket, and we would play all day throughout the project with other kids. When it unbelievably snowed in New Orleans back in December of 1963, we were at Josephine and Johnny's place.

Two good things I learned from my distant cousins: first, how to stand in the middle of the hallway and climb up the hallway walls while using your legs and feet to position your climb on the walls, one to the left side and one to the right side. The second thing I learned from my distant cousins was how to make "sugar water." If you have never had "sugar water," then you are missing out on one of the finer things in life.

Let's stop the introduction here and get to my experiences in Poplarville!

Herman Jr. and Naomi, where should I begin? Ha ha ha.

While at Josephine and Johnny's home one weekend, they decided to visit Poplarville, Mississippi, which was a norm for them on the weekends. Eventually, there were more weekend trips to Poplarville while Dianne and I were with them during the weekends. I was starting to enjoy those trips to Poplarville because we were out of the dirty, smelly house and because boys like adventurous things to do. It is just our nature.

So, there I was in Poplarville, back in the mid- and early sixties, "salt among pepper" and happy as can be. During those weekend visits, we would play in the yard, swim in the creeks, climb trees, throw things at the hogs and chickens, feed the hogs, ride horses, and, the best thing of all, we would get to ride in the back of a pickup truck. Life was good, and though there was hardly any food to eat, we did not worry about eating when we were playing or while we were swimming in the creek and having fun.

After those weekend visits, we would head back home to New Orleans on late Sunday afternoon, and I could not wait to go back to Poplarville.

Meet the Smiths

One weekend in Poplarville, we visited some of Johnny's distant relatives, the Smith family, who lived in another area of Poplarville. They were a large family of seven children: husband, wife, three boys, and four girls. Johnny's relatives started liking my visits with them, though I looked White when I stood next to the entire family, and I started enjoying being with their three sons. I thought the oldest was the coolest kid I had ever encountered up to that time in my life.

As time went on and our friendship grew closer, one weekend I asked their parents if I could come back and stay with them a week or two during the next summer. They said yes. That one-week initial visit led to two weeks, which led to three weeks, which led to three or four consecutive summer vacations in Poplarville, and still some weekend visits with my distant cousins.

My long summer visits to Poplarville, started when we lived in the Seventh Ward, around age eight when I was in the third grade. There I was, the little city slicker, the light complexion Creole boy spending all his summers in "the country," working the fields, feeding hogs and pigs, riding horses, swimming in the creek, diving from trees, and riding in the back of the pickup truck. We did a lot of fun things in Poplarville.

The Smiths' home, between the years I stayed there, from 1967 to 1972, did not have the luxuries we presently have, or that I had back at home in New Orleans during that time. No air-conditioning, no real kitchen because there was no running water, which meant no bathroom either. So when it was time to use the restroom, a person had to go outside to the "outhouse." Can you imagine waking up in the middle of a hot summer night, ninety-six to ninety-eight degrees, pitch-black outside, no lights, and you are walking to the outhouse with a flashlight, hoping no animals are on the walking paths—like rats, coons, possums, rabbits? The biggest concern of all: You are hoping, when you open the outhouse door, a snake has not tucked into bed somewhere on the floor.

I hated this part of the experience: If someone had just used the outhouse right before you, can you imagine the odor when you opened the door, especially on a hot summer night? Sometimes the odor was so appalling in that small-box building that during the daytime, if I had "to go," instead of going into that smelly outhouse, I would go off into the woods, dig a hole, then cover the hole very well after use, so that no one would know I had been there.

Confused Man

One extremely hot, sunny afternoon while riding in the back of the pickup truck, we stopped at a small grocery store to pick up some snacks—soda, chips, and cookies. There in the store were these White, middle-aged gentlemen just sitting around, talking and socializing. One of them was a very tall, heavyset gentleman. It looked as if he had just come out of the field because his jeans overalls were dirty, and sweat was running down his forehead.

He kept staring at me as he sat there on a chair in the air-conditioned store—just as the lady had stared at me that day my mom took us to the A&G Cafeteria. He could not keep his eyes off me. Eventually, he built enough courage to ask me a question. It went something like this: *"He'a, boy, com he'a. Len me axe yo som'in."*

I looked at him, walked over without an ounce of fear, and let him ask his question.

Very slowly, with a confused look on his face, he began to talk as if he were trying to figure out how to ask his question. So very slowly he said, *"R ya from he'a?"*

"No," I replied.

"Well, wer da ya be from?"

"Naw-lins," I replied.

"Oh, I nose ya could na be from roun' he'a. Dae don' look like ya round he'a."

After he said that, he looked over to the store owner behind the counter, started to laugh, and said to him, *"I toles y'all he wa na from roun' he'a."*

Let me interpret for you what he really wanted to know; it probably would have sounded something like this: *"He'a, boy, who bee's yo mama, and who bee's yo daddy?"*

He knew I was mixed; I'll give him that much credit. The Smiths' oldest son, who happened to be driving the truck that day, just ignored the gentleman and hustled us all together before something bad would be said or happened. We purchased our items and headed out of the store.

Swimming and Whipping

One thing I loved about Poplarville was swimming. Those summer days were always hot, and the home I stayed in did not have air-conditioning or running water, so a visit to the ponds and creeks was a daily ritual in the summertime. Yes, there were snakes in the water, but it never mattered to us young kids because we did not imagine accidents could happen. We sure were not going to allow a snake or snakes to keep us from swimming in the pond or creek. But, before we dove into any pond or creek and started swimming, we had a plan of how to get rid of the snakes.

We would stand on the ridge of the creek or pond and start stirring up the water with large tree branches. This would scare off the snakes in the area. If a snake came up to the top of the pond or creek, we would whack it on the head and kill it with one of the sticks or branches. Yes, it was that simple. I know it sounds strange, but we did it; a couple of times we had to kill some snakes before swimming.

We had a couple of special spots to swim, either the somewhat-clear creek in the woods or the dirty, muddy pond. The creek was always cleaner than the pond, and because there was no running water at the house, when it was time to bathe, we often visited the creek, which was a superior alternative to standing up in a metal tub in the middle of the house.

I was always too smart, even for myself sometimes. One extremely hot day, I wanted to go swimming, but Mrs. Smith said no one was to leave the house until the adults got back from running their errands. On that day, my ego and city-slicker demeanor got the best of me. No one was going to tell me I could not go swimming. No, not anyone, because swimming was my only purpose for wanting to visit Poplarville every summer. It was hell hot in the unair-conditioned, old, wooden home that had a tin roof soaking up the sun, making it even hotter. Besides that, the adults were taking exceedingly long to get back, and I was getting very impatient. So, I encouraged Mrs. Smith's younger son Lester and my cousin, who was also visiting that week, that we should just leave, before the adults got back, and go swimming.

Lester's three sisters kept telling Lester and my cousin not to listen to me—that if they did, they would end up in big trouble. I kept on, over and over, trying to convince those two innocent youngsters that we should just leave and go swimming and try to get back before the adults. Once I convinced the two knuckleheads to follow my advice, the three sisters interfered. We had a major quarrel and started screaming back and forth at each other. But like two foolish little kids, Lester and my cousin listened to my unreliable wisdom and allowed "the blind to lead the blind." We gathered up our stuff and took off out of the house to go swimming.

As we walked away, Lester's three sisters were standing in the doorway screaming, *"Y'all gonna git it; I gonna tell Mama. Oooooh...y'all gonna git it."*

We continued to walk and did not pay attention to those "stupid" girls, as we often called them. We would say, *"I ma not studden bout y'all."* So, I achieved my goal of wanting to swim that day, and I had two innocent victims to support my rebellious initiative, so swim we did. The water was nice, cool, and flowing swiftly through the creek. Later that day, water was going to flow swiftly out of our eyes for the three of us.

When we arrived back at the home from our swimming adventure, we saw the truck in the front yard, so we knew the adults had arrived back before us. As we were getting closer to the house, we could see Mrs. Smith standing in the doorway. She was a large, dark complexion woman with a beautiful smile. She usually had one the most beautiful smiles in the world, but on this day, she did not have a smile on her face. She was always so sweet and one of the most devoted Christian people I have ever known in my life, but on this day, "the spirit was willing, but the flesh was weak."

I had never seen Mrs. Smith so upset or angry. She was always cool, calm, and collected. She would never let anything upset her, but this was the day something else was aggravating her, and she was ready to put an end to the problem. She seemed to have been standing in that doorway for a while because sweat was running down her neck, and the top of her dress was wet. Why was she so upset? All we did was go swimming and bathed as we had done every other day.

She just stood there in the doorway, looking at us as we approached. None of us said anything to each other as we got closer. We kind of knew what was about to happen. When we arrived at the front door, we stopped and looked up at her.

All she did was make a gesture with her arm and pointed towards the big bush about fifteen yards to the left of the front door.

I stood there, not moving, and watched as Lester turned and walked over to that bush, pulled off a branch, and came back. My cousin followed behind him and ripped off a branch too. I just stood there, playing stupid, as if I did not understand her gestures. I was trying to play a mind game with her as she glared at me.

Then she screamed, *"Don cha make me come down dem stairs and go get one fa ya, especially you!!"* She had been fully informed by the girls that I was the instigator of the swimming adventure.

Since we were fearless enough to disobey her rule that no one was to leave the house without her permission, I figured giving us the liberty to choose our on branch meant that we were brave enough to take the lashing she was about to put on us. Lester was first for the scalding; my cousin was second.

As I watched those two kids get the hell beat out of them, I wished I had run first to that bush, picked a branch, and gotten this scalding over with, because as I watched, every time she whacked them, I felt the torment mentally. I stood there, not moving, wishing this day had never happened.

After Lester's and my cousin's blistering, she turned to me. All I remember was the pure hell of every whack. Where were my two angels, Mercy and Grace?

After that beating, the three of us we went outside to find a cool spot under a shaded tree to cool our bodies off. We started comparing and counting the welts on our legs, as if we were military soldiers comparing medals and stripes. We wanted to see who was whacked the most. Trust me, I had the most strikes, and those showed more noticeably on my high-yellow skin.

You learn a lesson once and only once, and if you're smart, you can use that lesson when making future decisions. I learned a real-life lesson that day, and I never disobeyed any of her instructions after that chastisement. Moving forward in my life, all adult instructions outside of my family were just as important.

The Taste of Watermelon

I learned a lesson about watermelon, too, in Poplarville, and that is, it can be eaten for breakfast. I had never eaten watermelon for breakfast, ever, until those summers in Poplarville.

Eating watermelon for breakfast in Poplarville was as normal a thing as eating hot cakes or cereal. You may think it's strange, but we ate watermelon just about every day in Poplarville, Pearl River County, Mississippi—the watermelon capital.

There are days when I am mentally consumed with my business affairs or personal matters, and my experiences in Poplarville can be the farthest things from my mind or thoughts. As soon as I bite down into a piece of watermelon, however, like magic, my memory of those experiences resonates. Every time we eat watermelon, I tell my wife, *"This watermelon tastes like Poplarville, Mississippi,"* and she laughs.

Ripe, warm watermelons are so delicious, just about as delicious as ripe pumpkins, or should I say, sweet as Pumpkin.

Pumpkin—My First Kiss

Time to go to church. Revival!

I am not with Grandma Valetta whom, often hauled us to church. I am in Poplarville. On those hot summer nights, one thing country folks do, and that is, go to church. We would attend church about two or three times a week, at night, during revivals and then ALL day on Sunday.

When attending church services, I noticed this pretty little brown-skinned, brown-eyed girl everyone called Pumpkin. I never knew her real name. After church services, we would play outside a little while before going home. I was told by one of the other girls after one of the church services that Pumpkin liked me, and she wanted to get to know me. I was just a middle age kid at this time so girls were an unknow entity for me.

One late evening, right before the sun went down and before attending revival, we (all the Smiths' kids and some other kids who lived close by) were all dressed up and ready to attend church services and were socializing out on the dirt road away from the front door of the house. We were waiting to be called back to the house to jump in the back of the truck to go to church. There were about twelve of us, seven girls and five boys, just goofing off and hanging out on this dirt road on this hot late-summer evening. Pumpkin was among the group of girls.

One of the girls came up to me and said, *"Pumpkin wanna kiss you."*

I asked the girl, *"What?"*

She repeated, *"Pumpkin wanna kiss you."*

Oh my God. Fear took over my entire body. I had never kissed a girl before. Obviously, Pumpkin was more aggressive than I was because she knew what she wanted. We boys were not even thinking about touching or kissing anyone of those girls that evening. We were just waiting to go to church.

That girl told all the boys that Pumpkin wanted to kiss me, so the boys started teasing me and saying, *"Man, ya gotta do dis. Ya a punk if ya don't kiss ha ."*

Trust me when I tell you I was scared as hell. I did not want to do it, and I contemplated back and forth and tried to put it off for the longest time. After all we were on our way to church!

I may go to hell for kissing this girl.

But the other girls and Pumpkin insisted that the kiss had to happen. I was just standing there in fear of death, and the boys were behind me, verbally harassing me to kiss this girl. The girls and Pumpkin approached me, and then they stopped. She stood about four feet in front of the girl group. All the boys were behind me. I stood about four feet in front of the boy's group, facing Pumpkin. About five feet separated Pumpkin and me. I could not get the muscles in my body to move my legs towards her.

Everyone kept chanting, *"Kiss, kiss, kiss, kiss!"*

I could not move. I stood there, frozen like a block of ice. The boys started pushing me, and my feet started to slide in the dirt towards her; she was just standing there with her cute little face. As the boys kept pushing me into a closer position, directly in front of her, I tried to catch my breath. At that point, some of the boys started calling me names; true, I was scared as hell. I thought we were supposed to be going to church!

What if I kiss this girl and then I die tonight? I am going straight to hell.

I was scared. The pressure was getting heavy, but I had to do this, or I would be called a punk or a sissy, and that was worse. So, I got the nerve to do it. I seized my Mack Daddy position, went up to her, put my arms around her back, and we locked lips. I had no idea what I was doing; I had just gone from wimp to Mack Daddy in a New York second, and I was kissing a girl for the first time.

As I was kissing Pumpkin, I felt an arousal sensation happening in my body. I had never felt anything like that before. At that point, the boys started pushing on my back and head; and the girls began doing the same to Pumpkin. They kept pushing us together, but that was not necessary because we were already kissing. We could not get any closer than we were, but because those kids kept shoving us, we could not relax and freely enjoy the end of the kiss. We were thrust together so forcefully that our bodies were touching, and we could not move. I did not want her to feel those rocks in my pants because this was a new thing for me too. I remember that our lips were smashed together so tight that I could literally feel her teeth pressed up behind her lips. We did not open our mouths—no saliva, no tongue—just lips.

The kids finally stopped pushing us together. We stepped back from each other and just stood there. The silly kids were acting as if their football team had just won the Super Bowl. They were celebrating as if there were a happy ending to this event. But, because of our friends' silly behavior and the physical commotion caused by their pushing us together, what should have been a very pleasurable experience turned into disappointment. Pumpkin did not want to kiss again, so it was probably just as awful for her as it had been for me. See, God did intervene; knowing we were on our way to church, He kept us from sinning.

After that "pushing kiss," I never wanted to kiss a girl again in my life—at least, not at that time. I eventually had a conversation with one of the older Smith boys about that sensation feeling I had during the body-mashing event; in reply, he gave me my first "street" lesson about the birds and the bees. Oh, Mom, now I know, what things a man and a lady do...ho, ho, ho.

After his instructions, I was thoroughly well-informed and ready to exercise what he had explained to me. I prepared myself emotionally. If I was ever offered the opportunity to kiss another girl, I would man up, and transform into my Mack Daddy character.

The Horse—Mercy And Grace

As a ten- or eleven-year-old boy, while in Poplarville, there were numerous first, and second, and thrid time experiences. This next experience, allow me to avoid injury or death on a hot summer day.

There in Poplarville, on a blistering-hot summer day, I was standing at the end of an imaginary finish line, waiting to declare who would be the winner of a race between a horse and a Shetland pony. Looking up the red-dirt road about two hundred yards, where two kids were saddling the two animals, I was just standing there, as any kid would do, waiting and waiting. There was nothing to do and nothing to worry about—no snakes at my feet, no bugs biting me—nothing to do but just wait for those two knuckleheads to cross the finish line.

Suddenly the race starts, and the two riders are heading towards the finish line. As I am standing there watching the race, when the animals are about one hundred yards away, maybe it was just my mind playing tricks on me—or maybe my two angels, Mercy and Grace, are already starting to warn me—but the horse seemed to be directing all of his attention towards me. So I began cautiously focusing my attention back on the horse as the race gets closer to the final line where

I am standing. For some strange reason, the horse's eyes and my eyes are locked on each other.

Unexpectedly, the horse veers out of the middle of the red-dirt road, and the rider cannot pull him back. The horse gallops straight towards me.

Is it my light complexion? Is it my hair? Why is the horse running full throttle and coming directly at me? Maybe I should not have kissed Pumpkin: I'm I being punished?

I can see the rider has lost control of the horse and is now holding on for his dear life. At about thirty yards away from me, I conclude that the horse will trample and crush me. So I immediately turn around and start running on the edge of the road as fast as I can, looking for a safe place to hide and block myself off from the horse. A slight distance ahead of me, I see an empty eighteen-wheeler flatbed trailer sitting on side of the road. The horse is about twenty yards behind me, and the rider cannot stop him. I had to make a quick decision.

My first and only thought to prevent myself from being trampled was to get deep under the flatbed trailer. If the horse didn't stop, he would run into the top of the trailer because he is too tall to run under it. The horse was about ten feet behind me when, while still running, I literally leaped forward with all my strength, arms first, and dove under that trailer like Superman, landing in the red dirt under the trailer on my chest and stomach.

The horse slowed down just in time, slightly bumping into the trailer while the rider was still holding on for dear life. The horse was directly behind me as I dove, so as my body landed under the trailer, my right leg was not fully under it. The horse's hoof came down and grazed me, scratching the back of my right ankle. When the horse came to a full stop, the kid who was riding fell off, hitting the ground and ending up with more bruises from the fall than I had.

I don't know why that horse wanted to trample and possibly crush me. The kid riding the horse said he was scared because the horse would not stop; he thought it was going to run into the trailer. That was a close call with death that day.

The Panther—Mercy and Grace

Another possible close call with death came one late-summer of 1971. This would be my last summer vacation in Poplarville. Mrs. Smith told my mom I was getting older, meaning I was too much for her to handle along with her other seven kids. And not only that, I was also a handsome young man, she said, and she told my mom the girls in the area kept visiting the house for no reason. Are you sure, no reason, Mrs. Smith? I was about twelve years old at that point, and yes nature was taking its course.

One Sunday afternoon, we were visiting with some neighbors and friends on the east side of Poplarville, at a home of a young lady with whom I shared interests. The Smith boys decided to head home before dark. They advised me to either follow or accompany them, but I had other intentions, more important female intentions, since I was older and knew about the birds and the bees. So, they left me behind to walk home by myself.

The young lady I was interested in was out on the porch of the home, I visited with here for a short stay, just socializing and having a good time before her parents called her into the house. That meant it was time for me to leave, and I had an unusually long walk back to the house, alone, at that, and in the dark.

I started heading back to the Smiths' house on the blacktop road, and it was almost pitch-black, except for the bright, full-moon's light. There was only one light pole on the long road, and that light pole was in front of the church we attended many nights. I'd never thought much about that light pole before, but as I was walking in the dark, I realized why that light pole was in front of the church. Without it, we would not be able to see in the parking lot of the church at night after services.

I was walking on the right edge of the road, and there was a cornfield on the left side. As I passed the church, I heard something moving in the cornfield. Whatever was in that corn pasture was moving anxiously, and I started moving anxiously too. The movement in the cornfield sounded as if it were occurring right under the light pole in front of the church. I stopped under the light pole and stood there, trying to see what was moving. Whatever was in the corn pasture stopped when I stopped. I stood there a little while longer and then made up my mind to start heading home again, moving north on the right edge of the road.

I am entering a darker area of the road, and whatever is in that cornfield starts moving again. I stopped; it stopped. I stood there in the dark, waiting to hear the movement in the cornfield again, and thought, *It is too dark where I'm standing. I'm going back under the light.*

So, I walked back toward the light pole; the sound moves back toward the light pole too. I cannot see what it is, and I am getting a little scared because when I stand still under the light pole, it does not move. I cannot see what it is, but when

I move north on the road towards the dark area, it moves with me because I can hear the corn stalks hitting each other. Also, whatever is in that cornfield is starting to make funny sounds that I've never heard before. I am really scared as hell. I think it is a wild hog, but I'm not sure.

Standing there, scared to death, I decide to try and make a run for it. I run for about twenty yards, and it moves swiftly in the cornfield those same twenty yards.

I am terrified. I stop, turn around, and run back under the light pole. I'm frightened now, and all I am thinking about is that I need to get to the house. I know it is late, and the Smiths are expecting me to be in the house before everyone goes to bed. I determined that I am safe there because the movement only occurs when I move towards the dark area of the road. I am about 300 yards from the dirt road that leads to the house. There are no lights on that 300-yard span; it is pitch-black, nothing but the moonlight and stars. As I am standing there, I start to think it out.

Now, if I must stay here all night, maybe one of the adults or the Smiths' older son, will get in the truck and come look for me. I am safe under this light, so they will see me standing here.

While standing there thinking of different scenarios of survival, I looked up ahead to the hilly part of the road about 1,000 yards beyond the 300-yard span, and I can see cars approaching. About ten to twelve vehicles are all coming towards me at the same time. The driver in the first car of this caravan is driving very slowly, holding up traffic.

Maybe some other church service let out late, and everyone left at the same time.

What event caused those cars to be approaching me at the same time, I didn't know, but the line of cars presented a fast solution to my problem. I decided to use those vehicles as a street divider between me and the cornfield. As soon as the first car arrived at my location under the light pole, my quick plan was to take off running as fast as the horse that wanted to trample me, keeping the cars between me and that animal in the cornfield. I waited and waited, and when the first vehicle was about twenty yards away, I took off for the races, running north on the right edge of the road.

My heart was beating fast, and I was running as fast as I was able to. I couldn't hear anything in the cornfield because of the noise made by the cars and trucks passing between me and the cornfield and whatever it is. The people in those vehicles must have been wondering what was wrong with that White boy running so hysterically in the dark.

I finally made it to the dirt road that leads to the Smith's home, and I had to run in pitch-black darkness on it for about another 400 yards to make it to the house. As I am still running desperately and scared out of my pants in the pitch-black darkness, a big bug flies into my eyes. It frightens me so much that I start screaming extremely loudly and waving my arms around violently, as if I were a terrified little girl crying out.

The Smith family are in the house up ahead, and they hear me screaming at the top of my lungs. The two sons jump up and run out of the house towards me, thinking they have to rescue me. When they reached me, they asked, *"Wass wrong? Is someone or somin attacking you?"*

I stop running, and as I stand there trying to catch the last breath I had left in me, I start telling them the whole story as we walk back to the house. They tell me the adults are sitting in the living room, worried and wondering where I was, not wanting to go to sleep before I got home. Then they inform me that their mom and dad told them the local authorities drove throughout the community earlier that day and warned the community that there was a sighting of a panther—a big black cat. They told everyone to be cautious, especially at night.

Now I'm really freaked out! Thanks a lot for the late news.

Those woods were the darkest woods I had ever been in during my life, and walking through them at night was not unusual for Poplarville boys. But to be chased by an animal was not normal for anyone, especially not this city slicker. I was glad this was my last summer in Poplarville because that incident was horrifying.

My family surprised me and came to get me that summer. I had no idea they were on their way that Sunday afternoon. I was outside slopping the hogs when they pulled up. I was glad to see them.

Chapter VII

The Eighth Ward—Saint Roch Community—and Ninth Ward

Now I Know

In January 1969, we moved to the Ninth Ward from Creole Village in the Seventh Ward. Law Street and Almonaster Avenue are the border lines of the Ninth Ward. The east side of Almonaster Avenue is the beginning of the Ninth Ward. We lived on the east side of Almonaster Avenue, on Law Street, directly next to the Almonaster Avenue Bridge. Coincidently my grandparents, Valleta and Gilbert moved into the same neighborhood a couple of months after us, only two blocks away, around the corner. They lived on Almonaster Ave.

When we moved into this neighborhood in the winter of January 1969, it was about ninety percent racially White. I was still attending Epiphany Catholic School, and my mom and now-stepdad purchased the home, their first, with a pool in the backyard! It was one of those aboveground pools about four feet high; nevertheless, we were the first people in our family to have a pool, and within my mom's social circle of friends and my and Dianne's friends and schoolmates, we were the only Black family with a pool.

This is the house we lived in on Law Street in the Ninth Ward.
It was destroyed by Hurricane Katrina in 2005.

Law Street and Almonaster Avenue

My first experience in this White neighborhood was truly a paradigm shift in my understanding and perception of the White class. Several of my experiences with my new White neighbors and White classmates would eventually enlighten me about the New Orleans Ninth Ward White culture.

During our first weekend in our new home, it was very cold and wintery; temperatures were below freezing. My mom, sister and I, were in the kitchen, and as I looked out of the kitchen window, I saw some White kids sitting over by the train tracks. They were not just sitting, but clowning around, goofing off, playing, and hanging out. I stared at them through the window for several minutes. I had never seen White kids play before.

As I continued to watch, I could not believe what I saw. Those kids, most were about my age and a couple seemed to be high schoolers, were smoking cigarettes. I told my mom to look and see if she noticed those kids were smoking cigarettes too. It puzzled me to see or watch these kids, my age level, smoking cigarettes in broad daylight where everyone could see them. I do not know where I developed the perception that White families were innocent and outstanding law-abiding citizens, but up to that point that is what I believed to be true. I thought White individuals around my age, ten to eleven, did no wrong. I thought all White people were clean-cut citizens who did no wrong. That thinking changed after we moved to Law Street.

I do not remember any talk of hatred towards anyone in our household when I was growing up; if there was, I did not pay attention to it. Therefore, I was this somewhat-innocent kid who could not comprehend these kids smoking cigarettes, because I knew that was a bad thing.

We, that is, the Creole/Black kids, at Epiphany and Saint Philip Schools, who were my age level or older, never thought of smoking cigarettes, and we sure would never have done it in public where everyone could see us.

My mom tried to protect her innocent, little Creole boy on this day as we both looked out of the kitchen window and watched those kids smoking cigarettes. She tried to persuade me that those kids had rolled up white paper into what looked like cigarettes, and they were just blowing cold air out of their mouths. Yes, it was a very, very cold January day.

Now, wait a minute, Mom, I am thinking to myself. *Thanks for trying to protect your fifth-grade son from smoking, but I am no fool. I know the difference between cigarette smoke and cold-air smoke blowing out of the mouth.*

She was trying to convince me to be a fool that day, but I knew without question that those kids were smoking cigarettes. Just to prove I was right, after those kids left that area where they were smoking, I went over there to see if there were any cigarette butts on the ground. There were many; that location was probably those kids' normal hangout for smoking.

I am sure when my parents decided to select this neighborhood to relocate to, they thought it would be a decent, nice, and family environment because there were White families living there. That was far from the truth. Those young, White Ninth Warders, smoking cigarettes was not the only bad thing they did. This new neighborhood was going to open my "little innocent" world to social realities, enlighten me about racial/social class differences and expose me to dangerous situations.

My Grandparents Gilbert and Valetta and My Bikes—Mercy And Grace

Gilbert and Valetta moved from their house on Clouet Street, the home where my grandmother and my aunt Melva endured Hurricane Betsy, to a two-story house on Almonaster Avenue, around the corner from our house on Law Street. It was a wonderful, large house with a garage underneath it. There was an apartment, on the bottom level and next to the garage, that they rented to an elderly White gentleman until he died.

For Gilbert and Valetta, purchasing this home was moving up in social class. Truly, from Clouet Street and its small, two-bedroom house that sat on large concrete pillars, they finally relocated to a larger home on Almonaster Avenue; it was three times the size of the Clouet Street home. Aunt Melva, in due course, would move into that apartment next to the garage on the bottom level.

My grandparents' home on Almonaster Avenue.

My grandparents would purchase me a bike every time I needed a new one. A new bike had only a one- or two-year life span with me as the owner. I would literally destroy all of my bikes because I rode them everywhere and every day. It took me about two years to destroy a new bike, not intentionally, but my bikes could not take the wear and tear of over usage every day.

As a kid in New Orleans, if you did not have a bike, you were lost; we would ride our bikes all over downtown and throughout numerous neighborhoods. A bike was a kid's means of transportation, and it gave him the freedom to get into trouble.

Throughout my early childhood, my grandfather personally felt that it was his obligation to take me shopping to pick out my bike, and he did an exceptionally good job at this. He enjoyed buying me bikes; and when those bikes needed repairs, he would perform those repairs down in his garage. It was our quality time together. He would show me how to fix what was broken. He would say, *"Red, come here! Let me show you how to fix this."* While we fixed my broken bikes,

Gilbert would take time to tell me about his bike-riding adventures and how far away from home he used to ride them. Now that I look back, it seems to me my grandfather enjoyed working on things in that garage, especially my bikes.

Gilbert also had a congregation of guinea pigs in the garage. Yes, a congregation, because those guineas pigs would reproduce so frequently that you could say it was like water flowing out of a faucet. I would play in the garage with everything he had in there—tools, guinea pigs, fishing rods, etc.

On one of our trips to purchase a bike during the summer of 1969, Gilbert took me to this bike shop right up the street from where my grandparents lived. He purchased me a nice, new, beautiful green bike. He never purchased used bikes; I always got a new one. I was so excited and ready to get on it and ride it out of the store, but it had to be assembled. The excitement of taking it home and assembling it was building.

It took my grandfather all morning to put together this brand-new bike. I just wanted him to hurry. As soon as he finished, I jumped on it, and I was off to the races—literally, off to a bike race.

"Bye, Daddy," I screamed as I took off. Yes, I always referred to me stepgrandfather as Daddy because he was the only man in my life who thoroughly understood what a father was.

I joined up with some friends in another neighborhood; they were racing their bikes up and down the one block of the street all day. They liked my new bike, and everyone wanted to ride it or race me.

Well, I started racing each of my friends, one by one, and I was kicking butt that day, winning every race. Later, in the afternoon, I rested for a while, and then it was time to race again. This one kid and I lined up at our imaginary starting point in the middle of the street.

"Ready…set…go!!!" screamed out one kid who was the designated starter of the race.

Down the street we rode, trying to out-pedal each other, when suddenly I lost control of my brand-new bike. I flipped over two or three times, then slid another fifteen to twenty feet, and came to a stop. I believe my two angels, Mercy and Grace, surrounded me with their wings because, the way I flipped headfirst a couple of times, I could have easily broken my neck. Instead, I had no major injuries, just some minor and major scratches and bruises, but that was not my greatest worry.

My greatest worry was that I could not believe I had just destroyed a brand-new bike my grandfather had purchased that morning. Remember, he took his precious time and assembled it piece by piece. I was anxious and scared, and more worried about how he would feel that I just destroyed the brand-new bike.

The bike was in terrible shape. The pedals were broken, as was the part that holds the pedals in place. The frame of the bike was bent out of shape, plus the brand-new paint job was ruined.

The other kids helped me up, and as I was walking the bike back to my grandparents' house, I was crying, nervous, and certainly scared. Neither my grandfather nor my grandmother had ever in the past given me a spanking or punishment of any kind. I just knew this was the first time they were going to be really upset, and I was imagining all kinds of horrific punishments I was about to receive.

Honestly, I prepared myself for a big punishment because I thoroughly deserved it.

In the distance, there stood the big house, and my grandfather and grandmother were sitting outside on the porch, which was on the second floor. Gilbert and Valletta could see me in the distance, walking the bike back home, so they knew something was wrong. They probably thought it was just a flat tire because that happened quite often. When I got to the front of the house, my grandfather came down the stairs to see what happened. My grandmother stayed on the second level, looking over the front railing of the porch.

As my grandfather got closer to me, while I stood there holding the bike up, he could see that the bike was damaged beyond his repairing abilities. He just stood there and looked at it. I remained silent as he examined the damage. After a few minutes, I began explaining what happened. Gilbert remained quiet and did not say a word as I continued to describe the entire incident. After I finished justifying the accident, I was waiting for an irate response from him.

But he just looked at me; then with one of the most peaceful facial expressions I'd ever in my life seen, he said, *"Dirty Red, accidents happen; they just happen. Do not worry about it. I can't fix this, but we will take it to the bike store tomorrow to get it fixed."*

That was one of the most wonderful things I had ever heard in my life—"accidents happen." It was as if the world had been lifted off my shoulders. I started crying, rolled the bike into the garage, and followed my grandfather upstairs to the porch.

I explained to my grandmother what happened. She just hugged me, and I finished crying in my grandmother's arms. She caressed me on the back and on my head and said, *"Thank*

God you are alive. It could have been worse. You could have died from a head injury or broken an arm or leg."

The next day, we took the bike to the bike shop.

After that accident, I indeed appreciated all my present and future bikes. I never took another bike for granted and did not have another bike accident. I was more responsible with all my bikes after that incident.

Attacked by Neighbors' Dog—Mercy And Grace

In our Law Street neighborhood, I made acquaintances with one of the kids who lived around the corner. He was not one of the kids smoking cigarettes on that cold January day. This kid was more of a nerd, a homebody. He had an older sister who was educated and sided with the liberal hippy theory that was sweeping the country through the flower-child movement. She would visit our home sometimes to hold intellectual, racial, and political conversations with my mom. We, both families, were trying to act "civilly" amidst the tense political environment of 1969.

One hot summer night, I was carrying the trash can from our backyard to the curb for the next day's garbage pickup, and I saw several dogs roaming free. I recognized one dog, and I knew it belonged to this kid and his sister, around the corner from our home. I'd petted that dog several times when visiting my friend at his home, and during those physical encounters with the dog, it never exhibited any aggressive tendencies.

On this night, while I performed my trash-can chore, I assumed the dog's owners did not know their dog was wandering free because I had never seen the dog away from their home. After placing our trash can in its place, I decided to escort the dog back to my neighbors' home. I called out the dog's name, he ran towards me, and I told him to go home. He turned to go home, and I followed him to their home, to let the family know he was roaming free and to make sure he got safely home.

As soon as the dog and I reached the front of the family's home, he turned around and started barking and snarling at me as if he were protecting their home from an intruder. I stood there for a couple of seconds, not thoroughly grasping why the dog had started barking at me. Then he started to attack me, so I turned to run, but it was too late. He jumped towards me and buried his teeth deep into the back of my left leg. I yelled and pulled away. Then he turned around and started running back to the house as if he had seen something. Maybe it was Mercy and Grace pulling him off me. The bite made a large tear in the back of my left leg, and because I pulled way, my flesh was literally hanging about one inch out of the wound.

I screamed, long and loud, until every neighbor in every nearby home heard me, which prompted all of them to look out their windows or open their front doors to see me crying and limping back to my home. I still have a scar today; that is how bad that bite was.

The daughter of the family immediately rushed to our home and tried to console my mom, frantically apologizing repeatedly, but there were no words to characterize why a dog would attack someone it knew. After my visit to the Saint Claude General Hospital Emergency Room that night, we ended our open communications with that family. The daughter, however, tried to visit a couple of times, but my mom was not as cordial as she'd been on her previous visits. The young, liberal-minded hippy eventually discerned my mom's negative body language and tone of voice; her frequents visits stopped.

Attacked by Bees—Mercy And Grace

In the summer of 1969, I had another tragic accident, but not while riding my bike and not by animal attack. Rather, this time it was with a swarm of honeybees. I was attending summer camp at Saint Philip the Apostle Catholic School for a couple of weeks. Like most summer camps, the workers took the students swimming during the hot summer months. Some of those swimming trips happened to be at the Saint Joseph Seminary over on the North Shore, Covington, Louisiana. I had been there before on another occasion when I was an altar boy at Epiphany. While there with the Epiphany altar boys, our director took us on a hiking trip through the woods.

On this new visit to Saint Joseph's, I kept bugging and begging the camp director to take us boys hiking through the woods, but he would not give in to my request. As the other kids started begging and asking him too, he changed his mind and gave in. In hindsight, I wish he hadn't given in.

We entered the woods and started walking and running through the woods, having a good time. I kind of got ahead of the group on this walking path. As the brave one, I shouted, *"Follow me,"* to all the other kids and the camp directors. Those knuckleheads did—the blind leading the blind.

Suddenly, I heard a loud noise above my head. I had never heard that sound before, nor did I know from where it was coming. It was a very loud and strange sound. I stopped walking and stood there trying to figure out what that sound was. All at once, like a bolt of lightning, I started to feel pain, as if stickpins were being pushed into my back, arms and legs, and those stickpins started to hurt awfully bad. Next thing I knew, that sound was a swarm of yellow-jacket bees attacking me. I started running like the racehorse in Poplarville, and crying like a baby who had just been dropped on his head. I was stung about twenty-five or thirty-five times. Two or three other kids had only one or two stings. Me, the ringleader, got stung the most.

I remember one of the counselors saying, referring to me, *"And he was the main one that kept begging us to go hiking in the woods."*

The camp director was certainly scared because he thought I would develop some type of infection, massive swelling, or possibly a high fever and even die. Believe it or not, the only discomfort I had were those physical stings. No infection, no swelling, no fever. It was amazing—it had to be a miracle. Now I know why the lady in church was holding my arm up. She was praying for me, right?

When I got home and told my mom and grandmother what happened, they could not believe it either because after I told them the entire story, as usual, I went outside to play and ride my bike that same afternoon.

Integration Child

Those bees and that dog attack may have hurt me physically, but those incidents cannot be compared to real "emotional damages" that I would eventually start to experience and comprehend during future events related to social, racial, and political cultural differences.

As I mentioned earlier, moving into a White-majority neighborhood in January of 1969 would change my entire ten years of social knowledge and experience. In the fall of

1969, my mom decided to use me as the integration child by sending me to a White-majority school. I was the first person in my family to attend school with White kids. That school was Our Lady Star of the Sea Catholic Elementary School, on Saint Roch Avenue. I was enrolled in the sixth grade with four other Black students. There were only six Black students out of a student body of abut 250, so my sixth-grade class was over three-quarters of the Black enrollment in the entire school. The only other Black student in the entire school was a Black girl in seventh grade. I had to explain to all the White kids that I was Black because they thought I was White. In the school, there were a couple of kids of my skin complexion who classified their race as White.

The first thing that astounded me while attending this school was the way these kids articulated their words and their unique use of some terminology that I had never heard. They used terms like "freak," "fruit," and "faggot" to slander each other. What was a freak, fruit, or faggot? What the hell was that? Black kids slandered each other with words like "sissy" or "punk."

These kids during lunchtime and after school where the wildest and rudest people I had ever met. I must admit, I was tough on those spoiled, arrogant, Seventh Ward "Creole kids" who attended Epiphany, but the kids in this school were nothing nice. These students shattered my interpretation of the Caucasian race.

Again, as I explained earlier in this book, my perception of White individuals at an early age was that they were decent, law-abiding citizens who respected each other, wanted the best things out of life, and never did anything wrong. Maybe the nurse with the "yellow hair" and the doctor who tended to me when I burned my hand and the nice people who rescued my sister from the bottom of the pool and taught us how to swim in Miami gave me that false impression. Maybe they were the exceptions.

Our Lady Star of the Sea Catholic School and Church,
Saint Roch Avenue, New Orleans, Louisiana.

These Ninth and Eighth Ward White kids at Our Lady Star of the Sea were mean, ruthless, and tough. Fighting was customary, and name calling—well, let's just say they used no words other than those needed to slander each other. My world had been opened to something I had no idea about. But there I was, every day in school, inundated with hatred, arrogance, and racism. I just learned how to deal with each day, good or bad.

One day at our home, my sister and I got into an argument, and I called her a fruit and a freak. My sister and mom stared at me with the strangest looks on their faces and asked me to repeat what I just said; because they had never heard that terminology either. So, I repeated it. They asked where I'd heard those words and how I'd learned to use them in a sentence.

To make a long story short, after I explained that my new school environment and the students of the Caucasian race introduced me to those terms to slander each other, we started laughing and shrugged it off.

My Seventh-grade picture, Our Lady Star of the Sea.
I'm in the bottom row, second from the right.

Trying to Pass

There are certain things or situations in life you can laugh off, but this next experience was no laughing matter.

As time went on while enrolled in this new school, I started to conform to my social environment and picked up on some terrible behavioral habits. I started hanging out with some kids at school and in the neighborhood; therefore, I learned my first lesson about trying to racially "pass" for something I was not, meaning attempting to identify as a White individual.

A Creole friend from the Seventh Ward and Epiphany School, Tony, was also attending Our Lady Star of the Sea Catholic School. He liked a girl named Ann, a girl in the fifth grade. Tony was a very light complexion Creole kid too, and he told Ann that his race was White. At that age, eleven, I did not fully comprehend the consequences of "trying to pass," claiming to be a race that you are not.

Among fair-skinned Creole/Black individuals, "passing" was big in New Orleans before the sixties and before the Black Power movement was launched. I can recall listening to a story told by a retired elected politician, a very light complexion Creole/Black mayor of New Orleans. He explained in detail to a group of us about how, back in the fifties, as a young adult, he'd "passed" several times, trying to catch a cab ride home late at night from uptown to downtown.

Whenever Tony was with his little White girlfriend and the race subject would come up, I would let him take the lead; I never corrected him. I was a thoughtless, stupid little follower. I never thought about it because at the time I did not completely realize that what he was doing was wrong.

Honestly, you are not guilty of breaking a rule if you don't know it exists. But once you have been told about the rule, and you knowingly break it, you are automatically in the wrong.

This naïve sixth grader did not know that trying to pass was a real, terrible issue, especially in my family. I honestly did not know it was wrong, at least not yet, and I did not thoroughly grasp its social, emotional, and political ramifications, but I would soon find out.

One Sunday morning, my sister and I walked to Our Lady Star of the Sea Church to attend Mass. Most of the kids I went to school with attended church there too. Tony's girlfriend and another girl were walking in the opposite direction, approaching us.

Without thinking, I told my sister to tell them she was my cousin. How foolish of me to do that, but, again, I did not know it was foolish at the time; that is why I did it. It is amazing how, at the moment I saw those two girls, I did not remember I was Black. But, I knew I was Black when Tony would often tell everyone we were White.

Boy, I should have never told my sister to tell those girls she was my cousin. That was an unforgivable sin. My sister was mortified; she took off and ran home. Let's just say, after she described to my mom what I had asked of her, I very quickly became knowledgeable about my transgression at age eleven; I learned the consequences of trying to pass and asking my sister to belittle herself for my personal, social gratification. After my mom's "boisterous" verbal clarification description, let's just say I never tried or thought about passing again. Know the "truth" for the "truth" will make who you are.

As a high school student, a college student, and an adult, I have had opportunities to identify as another race other than Black, but have never done so. Even today, in this evolving political and social media bewilderment, people literally ask me what my racial identity is. Duh!!!

King-Cake Parties—Embracing Civility

Speaking of passing, how about the passing of a parade on "Fat Tuesday" or Mardi Gras day? The Mardi Gras season starts on the day of the Feast of the Epiphany, January Sixth, which is a couple of months before Mardi Gras Day. Christianity describes the Feast of Epiphany as the day the Three Wise Men, or Three Kings, arrived to visit the Baby Jesus, bearing gifts. A New Orleans social group called the Twelfth Night Revelers started the custom of hiding a bean inside the Mardi Gras king cake. Whoever found it in their piece of cake would be crowned the king or queen of the Mardi Gras balls. Later on, the bean was changed to a baby. The recipient is said to receive good fortune after finding this prize. That person is also supposed to host the next king-cake party that coming weekend and, of course, provide the next king cake. This process continues up until Mardi Gras Day.

While still attending Our Lady Star of the Sea in eighth grade, I was maturing rapidly, and party happenings were invading my consciousness. One of the students decided to give a king-cake house party, which at the time was something I had no knowledge of, and they invited us two or three Black kids. I learned that if you received the small doll baby that was inside one of the slices of cake, then you had to give the next king-cake party that coming weekend. The secret to not being responsible for the next weekend's party was not to eat a slice of cake. I can't describe to you the expressions on those parents' faces when we Black kids showed up in their home for the king-cake party. Those parents were in high school back in the '50's and 60's, therefore their values clarification paradigms are not as acceptable as that of their 70's off spring. Remember, this is '72, and things are not as pleasant as Dr. Martin Luther King Jr. so elegantly put it in his "I Have a Dream" speech. As far as we Black kids were concerned, we wanted to embrace that dream and walk in the spirit of Dr. King's words, that is why we showed up to their house party. But for my classmates' parents, back in 1972, those words were honestly a social and spiritual challenge; it just was not that easy for us to walk "hand in hand."

Eighth Ward — School Drop Outs

For some of us students, we were really trying to embrace change and progress and walk hand and hand, and for some other White guys in our Eighth Ward neighborhood, close to our school, they were trying to walk hand and hand with the girls in our school. These guys were drop outs, and many of them would hang out only one block from Our Lady Star of the Sea School, at a mom-and-pop store on the corner of North Johnson and Arts Streets.

All the boys in school tried to date the silly little girls that we attended school with, but those girls preferred the drop-outs who stood out on the corner and smoked cigarettes all day. For the life of me, I could not understand why those trashy-looking, dirty, long-haired, stinky, tattooed, dropout guys were more attractive to the silly girls in our school. Many of those girls would hang out on the corner after school with the dropouts.

One day, those same dropouts encouraged two of the girls in our classroom to skip school and hang out with them. When the principal and administrators of our school called the parents of those two girls and asked why they were absent, it was then determined that those two girls were actually supposed to be in school that day. The police eventually caught up with the two girls, and then, for some strange reason, their parents and the principal agreed to bring them back to school so we could see them. They brought those two girls into our classroom; they were dirty, stinky, and funky, and I was not impressed. Their odor that day reminded me of the smelly girl who was standing in front of me the night we integrated the Beach.

Lesbian Couple

There were some people, during the sixties and early seventies, who had "dropped out of society" or did not want society to know their true identities. I did not know while living on Law Street that the two very nice White ladies who lived across the street from us in a small brick double were a couple.

One of the ladies was tall, kind of heavyset, and had blonde, not yellow, hair that was cut short with a part down the left side. She never let it grow long; she kept it short. Her name was Ms. Peggy. The other lady was small-framed, but not skinny, short, and brunette; she was always smoking a cigarette. Her name was Ms. Brenda.

They were our neighbors who lived directly across the street from us, and they favored this Creole boy. They were genuinely nice ladies. My mom would speak and have nice neighborly conversations with them all the time. Those ladies thought I was the cutest little thing they'd ever seen.

One night, Ms. Peggy asked my mother if I could ride with her in her car as she took Ms. Brenda to work. My mother said sure; eventually, I would ride several times with Ms. Peggy when she took Ms. Brenda to work. I concluded Ms. Peggy did not want to drive home alone after dropping Ms. Brenda off at work.

On my first ride, Ms. Brenda placed a traveling-type hang-up bag on the back seat of the car next to me. She said they were her working clothes. I had no idea what type of occupation required her to bring her clothes to work in a traveling bag every night. Don't people wear their clothes to work? What was in that long bag? What did she change into while working at night that she could not wear in the car? And why did she go to work at night and not during the daytime like normal people?

The answer to my questions? Ms. Brenda was a Burlesque dancer on Bourbon Street!!!! I took that ride several times, and every time I got an eyeful from the back seat of that car when we would drop Ms. Brenda at the front door of the club on Bourbon Street.

Driving on Bourbon Street at night was legal back then. Today, Bourbon Street is closed to vehicle traffic from 7:00 p.m. until 5:00 a.m. We had to enter Bourbon Street from Canal Street, and Ms. Peggy had to drive four or five blocks up Bourbon Street to get to Ms. Brenda's club. Other cars in front of us would move at a very slow pace on Bourbon Street because the drivers and passengers in those vehicles were probably doing what I was doing, getting a "free look " into every nightclub that had the front doors open. There were several Burlesque clubs on Bourbon then, more than there are now.

Eventually we would get to the club where Ms. Brenda worked. As we stopped to let her out, my eyes would be glued to the front door of the nightclub, waiting for the doorman to open it so I could get another free look. Ms. Brenda would grab her bag off the back seat, kiss Ms. Peggy goodbye, and into the club she would go. As she entered the bar, I would watch her and anxiously wait for the doorman to open the door. When he did, I got an eyeful of natural, organic, human female curves every time.

After doing that night ride several times, my mom asked me where Ms. Brenda worked. I told her, and then my mom concluded Ms. Brenda was an exotic dancer. Darn, party rides are now over. I think my mom had a conversation with both ladies, and they thoroughly comprehended my mom's position respectfully, so the night rides to Bourbon Street ended.

Later that year, those two sincerely nice ladies probably apologized to my mom because she said yes when they asked to take me to a more child-friendly event—the Sugar Bowl parade on Canal Street.

Sugar Bowl Parade

New Orleans is the host city for the NCAA's Sugar Bowl football game every year. The game used to be played at the old Tulane University Football Stadium before the New Orleans Superdome was built. After the Superdome was built, Tulane Stadium was torn down, and both Tulane University and the New Orleans Saints played at the dome, until Tulane later constructed another smaller stadium on campus.

Tulane University's old football stadium, New Orleans, Louisiana.

The entire world knows that New Orleans is famous for Mardi Gras and extravagant parades, but a lot of people have forgotten that there was once a major Sugar Bowl parade, too, the night before the game. This particular year, the University of Arkansas was playing the University of Mississippi, also referred to as Ole Miss, the Ole Miss Rebels. Back in 1970, the year of this Sugar Bowl game, Ole Miss used the Confederate battle flag as an icon that characterized their team name—Rebels.

I was a naïve eleven-year-old at the time, attending Our Lady Star of the Sea Catholic School. I knew White and Black people still had some social differences, but, believe it or not, I had not yet mentally associated the Confederate flag with the social or racial differences in society.

The day before the Sugar Bowl parade, Ms. Peggy and Ms. Brenda came over and asked my mom if they could take me to the Sugar Bowl parade. My mom said sure. Again, I guess it was their way of making it up to my mom for introducing me to exotic dancers and Bourbon Street.

The next evening, I jumped into the back seat of Ms. Peggy's car, and off we went to the parade. Ms. Peggy and Ms. Brenda were honestly wonderful ladies, and they loved talking to me and pointing out different locations while we drove. We arrived at our location along the parade route, somewhere on Canal Street, close to Broad Street, and we sat down on the median's curb to wait for the parade. I do not remember seeing any Black families in that area of Canal Street, but that did not matter. I was at a parade, and I was having a good time.

After a long wait, the parade finally arrived. There were several all-White high school bands, one after another, and plenty of floats. Up ahead in the parade route, we could see the floats; two floats represented each school. First, came the University of Arkansas float. It was decorated maroon and white. It was a nice float, but it looked boring to me. While other people along the parade route applauded the decorative Arkansas float, I booed at it, and booed fearlessly and booed at the Arkansas cheerleaders who were riding on the float.

Ms. Peggy and Ms. Brenda looked at me and simply said I should cheer for Arkansas. I did not know why; those colors were boring and dull.

The crowds along the parade route were not that big; therefore, people on the floats could make eye contact with a few spectators. I remember the Arkansas cheerleaders on the float looking at me as I was booing them hysterically. They glared at me as if saying, "What is wrong with you?"

I continued to boo wildly, jumping up and down as I screamed; I was just having a good, innocent time as a small kid.

Ms. Peggy and Ms. Brenda asked why I was booing so loudly. I told them I did not like those plain maroon and white colors. That was a good enough answer for them. After that answer, they left me alone.

Well, a couple more bands passed, and farther back was the University of Mississippi float. Their float colors were red, white, and blue, and the float was literally beautiful, with all those Confederate battle flags. As the Ole Miss float got closer, I started cheering, screaming, and hollering.

Ms. Peggy and Ms. Brenda looked at me and asked me to please stop cheering. I could not understand why. Their float was decorated nicely, their colors were better than Arkansas's colors, and the big Confederate flag on the top of the float was just blowing in the wind beautifully. The Ole Miss float looked better than the Arkansas float that night.

Ms. Peggy and Ms. Brenda wanted to know why I was cheering like a crazy person for Ole Miss and not booing. I said it was because I liked those colors and the float. That was a good enough answer for them because they then understood I was a naïve kid and did not know what that rebel flag represented. I remember one male cheerleader for Ole Miss applauding back at me. He and I made eye contact as I cheered crazily for their float decorations.

The parade ended, we drove home, and the ladies dropped me at the front door. I think they had a conversation with my mom that night because, right after that, my mom educated me about the Confederate flag and what it represented.

But I still did not fully comprehend, still not yet.

My First Comprehension of Racial Tension

One day, a friend of mine from the old Seventh Ward neighborhood, Russell, was visiting with me. Russell and I played musical instruments in the New Orleans Recreational Department Marching Band, NORD. In chapter four, while attending Epiphany School for third, fourth and fifth grades, I learned to play the trumpet and read music. Russell, two other kids, and I were the first Black kids to play in the NORD band. So now, while attending Our Lady Star of the Sea School, which did not have a music/band class, I found a means to continue my musical skills up until eighth grade. The NORD band marched in the traditional Mardi Gras and holiday parades. Practice twice a week would take place at City Park Gym, located on the corner of Harrison Avenue and Marconi Drive.

On the day Russell was visiting with me, we decided to ride our bikes throughout my new Law Street neighborhood, and we agreed to go venture across the Franklin Avenue Bridge, a small distance from my home on Law Street. Neither Russell nor I had ever been in that area of New Orleans, so we two innocent Black kids chose to ride our bikes and conduct our own social examination of the area.

The Franklin Avenue Bridge's pedestrians and bike path is located in the middle of the bridge, rather than on either side. Russell and I rode our bikes over the bridge, and when we got to the north side of the Franklin Avenue Bridge, it was just as we expected it to be.

Right at the foot of the bridge was a, dazzling community with a bowling alley, theater, strip mall, bakery, gas station, and all the perks of middle-class White America. We did not feel out of place; it was 1970, and we are free American citizens just riding our bikes. We did not feel insecure or scared about this adventure because for us to get to NORD band practice, we had to ride the Canal Boulevard bus, get off at Harrison Avenue, then walk five or six blocks through the neighborhood of Lakeview to get to the gym. We never had a problem or encountered any racial harassment while walking to band practice; therefore, we thought riding our bikes north across the Franklin Avenue Bridge would provide us the same secure experience.

When we arrived at the bottom of the bridge on the north side, we rode our bikes around the immediate community right at the base of the bridge. We were amazed at how clean the area was, and we watched as kids and teens went in and out of the bowling alley. Those kids were watching us too. We started to feel a little uncomfortable as those kids stared at us, so we opted to head back home and started riding our bikes back over the bridge.

When we were at the top of the bridge, out of nowhere we heard some guys screaming, *"Go home, N******! Go home, N******! You don't belong over here! Go back where you came from!"*

We looked around, and at the right side of the bridge, there were some White teenage boys standing in the back of a pickup truck, screaming at us. Russell and I just stood in astonishment, not knowing what to say or do. We were trying to figure out what all the commotion was about.

Then the violence and hatred happened again. They started throwing sticks and soda bottles at us while continuing to scream. It happened so fast that we did not have time to run to the bottom of the bridge or duck behind our bikes. One of the bottles hit me on my right arm and ribs, and Russell got hit in the middle of his back while trying to duck.

Russell was so angry and furious that he wanted to retaliate. I was in shock and bewildered, but I did not get as upset or angry as Russell did. As I was standing there, I was trying to figure out why those kids hated us so much; we had not done or said anything that would have caused them to behave in such an ugly manner. I stood there holding my painful arm and rubbing my ribs. I could not figure it out.

Then, what just happened ignited in my head like a light bulb, and I started to comprehend what was happening. I ultimately put it all together as I kept hearing that awful outburst, *"N******, go home!!!!"*

Now I know!!!! At that moment, it all became clear. Suddenly, I knew what the Confederate flag was all about, and I wished I could have taken back all my cheers for Ole Miss the night of the Sugar Bowl parade. I knew why the blonde-haired lady in the A&G restaurant stared me down. I also wished I could take back the embarrassing moment when I asked my sister to say she was my cousin, when I tried to identify with something I was not.

I was not some White guy full of hate, throwing bottles and sticks, shouting the N-word at innocent, little, civilized Black boys just riding their bikes for fun. I was being emotionally degraded by people I did not even know. Me, of all people, who did not have a stroke of racism in my blood.

When we got back home, Russell was still boiling with anger. We informed my mom, and she explained to us about venturing into other neighborhoods without adult supervision. We were just two small, harmless Black kids riding our bikes, not causing any trouble, but we learned a huge lesson about society that day, without asking for it to be taught.

My First Job

I now had a comprehensive understanding of racism after that Franklin Avenue Bridge incident. My outlook about my friends at school and neighbors changed, and I stopped hanging out with many of those kids. Life for me continued to go on, and I started to focus on what was best for me. I was getting older in age, and I came to the realization that I could not go to neighborhood parties, the movies, or Pontchartrain Beach with empty pockets; therefore, I needed to find a job that was not throwing newspapers.

We knew a Black gentleman who owned a mechanic shop right up the street from Our Lady Star of the Sea School, on the corner of Franklin Avenue and Johnson Street. He hired me to clean the shop every Saturday morning. I would wake up, get dressed, jump on my bike, and go off to work at the shop. My duties were to clean up the place that had been terribly disorganized all week. My responsibilities were to put all the tools back in place, sweep, pick up trash, empty the trash cans, and wash the floors down so that the other mechanics and employees could start off with a clean shop on Monday mornings.

That was a good gig for me. I made five dollars every Saturday. That was big money back then.

Apprehended by New Orleans Police

While I was trying earn some extra money to embrace civility and walk hand and hand with each other, the New Orleans Police Department "embraced" me to the back seat of one of their cars.

My church/school, Our Lady Star of the Sea, had a school fair one weekend close towards the end of school, and the fair ended around 9:00 p.m. on Sunday night. I was in eighth grade. As I was walking home—through the ninety-percent-White neighborhood where we lived—I saw several police cars, with patrol lights twirling, at the foot of the Franklin Avenue Bridge. Silly me wanted to see "What's Going On" (Marvin Gaye, 1971). Therefore, instead of going straight home, I veered off my "protected path" and approached the police cars.

Before I got within two blocks of the commotion, I heard a gentleman say, *"Stop, and don't make another step."*

When you hear those words, there is only one thing to do, STOP.

Let me put this in perspective based on the social environment at that time. This is the spring of 1972; the Afro hairstyle is in, and I have a big one. The picture on the front of this book is my eighth-grade picture. Because of the big Afro, and thank God for it, people knew I was Black. Even the policeman, who was telling me to stop, had concluded I was Black based on my Afro.

I think stopping is the only option a young Black man has when a White policeman tells him to stop. This policeman showed up out of nowhere, behind me. He was probably hiding behind some bushes or around a house, and I did not see him as I was approaching this crime scene.

I put my hands up, and I did not turn around to look at him, nor did I say anything. I only weighed about one hundred pounds at the time—the Afro added two pounds...joke! Out of the corner of my eye, I saw this big shotgun—yes, shotgun, not handgun—so now I knew something terrible had happened. But I was not involved, so I stood there like a concrete statue, still not seeing the policeman's face as he patted me down, then grabbed me by the back of my pants, picked me up off my feet, and gave me an out-of-this-world wedgie. He pulled the back of my pants up into my crotch to the point that I was on my tiptoes. He then dragged this one-hundred-pound boy while still holding the shotgun in his left hand. The entire time, I could see the shotgun to the left of my head, so I was too scared to turn my head to see his face. When we got to the scene of the crime, he placed me in the back seat of a police car without an explanation. I did not know what the hell was going on; I was scared and shaking hysterically.

As I continued to look out of the window from the back seat of the cop car, a Black cop came over to the squad car and opened the door to get my personal information. He looked at me kind of funny after he opened the door, and then I heard him tell another cop, *"I thought that was a girl, with all that hair on his head."*

What an idiot. I am wearing an Afro hair style, you stupid Uncle Tom cop. It's 1972, Black Power Movement, remember? Oh no, that's right; I forgot...you're a pig!

I looked out of the window of the police car, and I saw some girls with whom I attended school with; they were standing and looking on with the rest of the crowd. Those same girls were at the fair earlier that night, and we'd hung out a little while together until it shut down.

If only I can get those girls to give me an alibi and say I was at the school fair. That would let the police know I was not here, at the scene of whatever crime has been committed.

I was still not aware of what did happen. I knocked on the window of the police car to get another cop's attention. He opened the door, and I told him, while pointing to the girls, that I was with those girls over there at the school's fair. I asked him to please go verify that with them, again pointing to the two girls.

He walked over to have a conversation with them to verify my statement. He then came back to the car and asked me to get out, which I did. Then he told me to get back in; he walked back over to the girls and had another conversation with them. Again, he came back and opened the door of the car and started to explain to me that the two White girls told him the last time they saw me was about four hours ago at the school fair.

Four hours ago? Duh? That would be about five or five thirty, but I was literally talking with them closer to the end of the fair around eight thirty. I left a little after nine, when they left.

The cop said their statement put me at the fair at around five, and he closed the door in my face. Now, he could have been lying; maybe they did provide him with a reasonable account of the time, which did not place me at the scene of this crime, but he had his own agenda, and he was not depending on their account.

Well, I just sat there for about thirty minutes, saying my last prayers and going crazy because I knew I was going to jail. And you know what happens to little Creole boys when they go to jail.

Two or three more cops approached the car; one of them opened the door and asked me to get out again. I got out and stood there; then I asked them to explain to me what was going on; they ignored my request. As I was standing there, I looked over in front of the car. There were several other cops, including the Black cop who thought I was a girl, about twenty yards away, talking to a Black kid who was handcuffed.

Eventually, the Black cop approached me again, and when we were face-to-face, he opened his mouth and angrily screamed, *"Go home, boy! You not one of dem. Go home right now."*

Wait a minute, I am thinking. I cannot believe this Black cop basically screamed at me, and now I am free. That's not good enough for me. I am thinking about the cop who apprehended me with the shotgun, pulled my underwear up the crack of my butt, dragged me to a police car, tossed me in the back of a police car, shut the door, and did not tell me why I was being apprehended. That is not good enough for me; my mom did not raise a fool. I wanted to know what happened early that night that got me locked down in the back seat of a police car for thirty minutes and had me mentally envisioning bad things happening to me in prison.

As I started to walk away, I looked around and saw another noticeably young White cop standing nearby. So I asked, *"Sir, what's goin' on?"*

Nicely and softly, he began to speak and said the Black kid whom they had handcuffed did not identify me as one of the perpetrators.

Then I said, *"One of dem, who?"*

The cop then explained that several teenage Black kids around my age stole a vehicle, went joyriding on Franklin Avenue, got into a chase with the cops, and then crashed the stolen vehicle into an electrical pole at the foot of the bridge. After the impact, they jumped out of the stolen vehicle and ran throughout the neighborhood, trying to hide and get away. By coincidence, the area where I was apprehended was the same area a couple of them ran into trying to escape.

While this young cop is being nice and considerate and explaining to me what happened, the bully Black cop, who rudely screamed at me to go home, starts approaching me and the young White cop, fast and furious. When he reaches us, he gets right up in my face, and this Uncle Tom Black cop has the audacity to try and give me some personal advice by telling me, *"Go get a haircut. I thought ya was a girl with all dat hair on ya head,"* while laughing and looking at the young White cop as if the White cop was going to agree with him.

To me, it seemed as if the young White cop was embarrassed, standing there as we had to listen to this fat, loudmouthed, egotistical, arrogant behavior from this stupid-ass Black cop. Personally, I think the young White cop wanted to be a long-haired hippy; he was genuinely kind and was probably stuck in a job right after high school that his dad wanted him to do. Concluding, I followed the dumbass Black cop's advice and went home and told my mom and sister what had just happened. True, and, yes, they could not believe it.

New Orleans at Night during the 70's — Municipal Auditorium

The reason I was walking home by myself, late at night after the end of the school fair, was because in New Orleans, back in the early seventies, the streets were basically safe to travel at night; there was no crime against young people. Just the basic verbal abuse from White teenagers in cars as they drove by now and then.

While in seventh and eighth grades, I attended the professional wrestling matches every Thursday night at the Municipal Auditorium. It was the gathering place for many kids my age, including several of my friends. The Auditorium, as we called it, was a building that could seat about six to eight thousand people. It is still presently located in (Congo Square), Rampart Street, right across from the French Quarter, in the Tremé neighborhood. That building is now abandoned and behind a fence in a park called Louis Armstrong Park.

I would walk from our home on Law Street and Almonaster to catch the bus on Franklin Avenue, and ride the Franklin Avenue bus to Saint Claude Avenue, and then ride the Saint Claude bus to the auditorium, and then take that same bus route ride in the opposite direction to get back home at ten or eleven at night after the wrestling match. I was eleven, twelve, and thirteen years old while riding the bus alone at night many times with no problem.

I never had a problem with anyone trying to abduct, mug, or rob me—really, not one incident. While attending the wrestling match, my friends and I would do more than just watch the event. We would venture throughout the auditorium—upstairs, downstairs, behind the stage, up in the ceiling—and open doors to other locations in the building that were off-limits to the public. At one time, I knew all sections of the auditorium as if it were my second home.

No MVP

School is ending in a couple of days, Spring, May, 1972. I will be moving onto high school. What I learned from attending Our Lady Star of the Sea Catholic School, other than every nasty word in the English language (worse than those used by Ms. Marie), and a discernment of racial disparities, was to participate in team sports. I not only played all three sports while in eighth grade, but also was captain of all three teams: flag football (quarterback), softball (pitcher and home-run leader), and basketball (point guard, team leading scorer). What can I say? In 1971/72, I was a baller, shot caller.

So why did I not get the MVP for boys' sports at the end of the school year during the sports awards banquet? According to the director of sports, in his opinion, this fat White kid, who only played flag football and softball for the junior team, was more of a dominant player at the sixth- and seventh-grade level than I was at the eight grade level. His comment was "the junior team would not have won the games they won without him." Well, the eighth-grade team would not have won the games we won if it had not been for me, especially the basketball games, in which the fat kid did not play basketball for the junior team. Duh!!!! Do I really need to express my opinion as to why I was not awarded the MVP?

The French Market: Summer of 1972

Summer time is here. The wrestling matches on Thursday nights were eating up all my money I earned on Saturday morning for cleaning the mechanic shop. I earned just enough cash, five dollars, every Saturday. I was getting older, hanging out socially, and going to school dances and parties on the weekend, I needed more money.

My mom knew this older Black gentleman who owned a fruit and vegetable stand in the French Quarter / French Market area. She convinced him to hire me, so he gave me a trial period.

Let me give you a little New Orleans French Market history.

New Orleans French Market, now the flea market.

Before the French Market turned into the abominable, repulsive, detestable flea market full of junk, the French Market was a place merchandised with an abundance of fresh fruits and vegetables daily. Local mom-and-pop grocery owners would make visits to the French Market early in the morning, daily and weekly, to purchase the fruits and vegetables they thought they would sell that day in their local corner store. These older mom-and-pop stores where basically big open rooms with shelving in the front of a home;

therefore, the big front rooms only had dry groceries and did not have the big, sophisticated freezers for frozen food or refrigerators to keep fruit and vegetables cold.

Back before the eighties, New Orleans had numerous mom-and-pop corner-grocery stores before the big retailers ran them off or out of business. I am not exaggerating when I describe this; there appeared to be a mom-and-pop store every two or three blocks in every neighborhood. When I lived in the Seventh Ward on Annette Street, there was Millers Grocery on the corner of our block, Annette and North Tonti Streets; then directly around the corner on the end of the block was another store at the corner of North Rocheblave and Allen Streets, and then right up the street from that store, on the very next corner of Allen and North Dorgenois Streets was another store across the street from Hardin Park.

It was like that in many neighborhoods throughout New Orleans, and the place to be from 5:00 a.m. to 7:00 a.m., before those mom-and-pop stores opened at 7:00 a.m., was the French Market's fruit and vegetable area. It was the common community gathering place every morning for mom-and-pop owners and vendors of each fruit or vegetable stand in the French Market.

The French Market was also a gathering place for the truck vendors who drove around selling fruits and vegetables throughout New Orleans neighborhoods, while they sang a song of their own unique rhythm:

I ga apples, n bananas

I ga wadamelon red to da rhine

I ga peaches, I ga dem grapes

I ga lettus, rad damatoes

A lot of people do not know this, but each fruit or vegetable vendor at the French Market had a specialty product that was unique just to that vendor; though some vendors carried or sold some of the same products, each vendor had a special product or, as I understand it today, a monopoly on a specific product.

There was a vendor gentlemen's agreement or honor code, and everyone respected it. Here is how that code worked. For example, the gentleman I worked for had a monopoly on okra. When the okra farmers would come in from rural areas, those okra farmers first went straight to the gentleman I worked for. He would purchase seventy-five to ninety percent of all the okra; whatever he did not buy first, the okra farmer would sell to other vendors. And that was the process that was followed by every farmer and vendor.

The vendor next to the gentleman I worked for had a monopoly on tomatoes. Tomato farmers would go to him first and sell to other vendors what was left. The vendor at the very entrance of the French Market that faces Canal Street had a monopoly on garlic. He would hang those garlic cloves on strings, twenty to thirty of them hanging from the ceiling railing.

The vendor I worked for also sold his okra to the A&P supermarket. Once or twice while working for this gentleman, he had another helper, and that helper and I would load up my boss's freight truck with bushels of okra, and then we would drive to the A&P freezer warehouse in Jefferson, Louisiana. Once there, we would unload the order and make it back by nightfall.

The fun part about working in the French Market on the weekends and during the summer was that I got to ride my bike to work every morning; I was up early and out of the house. I would get to the market about 7:00 a.m., just as the mom-and-pop owners were starting to head back to their stores. And not only was the purchasing of product taking place, but the latest gossip, social and political issues, and news were always being discussed. If you could hear some of the stories these store owners and vendors told every day, it would blow your mind.

The greeting between the vendors and mom-and-pop owners was so unique and special. Early in the morning, the common opening line was "Hey, baby." No matter what your sex was, how tall, skinny, or fat, White or Black, you were referred to as baby or sugar.

"Hey, baby, how yaw doin'… Okay, baby… I take care of dat, shugah."

The gentleman I worked for recognized that I was reliable and accountable, and he knew I valued my commitment to his business. Therefore, he started to appreciate that he really needed someone like me. I had passed his test, because the first thing I would do when I arrived every morning was grab a broom and start cleaning up, organizing the boxes and baskets, and throwing away trash that had accumulated the night before and early that morning during the mom-and-pop rush.

I now look back and conclude the experience I acquired while cleaning the mechanic shop prepared me for the French Market job because the trash in the French Market was ten times more every day, and the mechanic shop was only once a week. While I cleaned up every morning, the owner would refill the canisters or crates to prepare for selling that day. He started to appreciate and rely on me so much that during the summer of 1972, he started leaving as soon as I got there. So not only did I have to clean up the filthy place, but also I had to refill the containers for the selling table. Double duty!!! But it was fun because I got the chance to act and talk like a vendor. I even started referring to the customers as baby and sugar too. *"Hey, baby, can I help you… Okay, sugar…"*

I look back now and can comprehend the most important thing of all about that job was the fact that this owner trusted me with his money. I would sell about $300 to $600 a day during the summer of 1972. Do you know how much money that was back then? And God is my witness when I tell you this…I did not steal a penny.

None of the vendors had a real inventory system to track if someone sold $300 that day or $600. There were just a bunch of vegetables in crates on the back of the supply truck; I would refill the table from what was on the truck. My honesty surely made this gentleman feel content with me, and I felt at ease with him too because I was making ten dollars a day…cold cash…in 1972…and I was only a fifteen-year-old. That was big money!!!! But my earnings sometimes were based on how my boss's gambling results were for that day.

Gambling in the French Market

Most of the vendors who owned or leased the areas to sell their fruits and vegetables were compulsive gamblers. I did not comprehend the seriousness of gambling or how much money was being lost or won until one day when one of my boss's farmers arrived with a big truckload of okra. The gentleman I worked for negotiated that part of the business, but he was not around. I didn't know whom I could ask to go get my boss in the building across the street; that's where he and other gentlemen gambled. So, I asked the vendor who was working next to our section to watch our area while I went to get my boss.

I ran across the street to this warehouse-type building that had big freezers on the first floor where the vendors would store vegetables and fruits. There was a side door at street level, which led to the steps to the upstairs area where I knew my boss was. I entered, and in front of me was an old wooden-floor hallway; the walls on both sides were brick. The hallway was dark, dusty, and dirty, and as I reached the old wooden stairs and started up, I could hear the voices of the men in the room above. As I got to the door opening at the top of the stairs, I could see the room, which was smoke filled and hot as hell, and many vendors sitting at a table gambling. They were playing cards with tons of money on the table and Dixie beer bottles everywhere. The large widows that faced the French Market were open, so the light was shining through, and a light breeze was blowing in.

As I stood there, my boss looked over and saw me; he waved me over with his hand. I walked over to speak with him while looking at the loads of money on the table. I explained to him the situation; he said okay and told me to go back to the vending area to let that farmer know he was coming soon.

As I looked over to the table again while leaving, there had to be over $1000 to $2000 on that table because all I saw were tens, twenties, and plenty of one-hundred-dollar bills in a cluster. The boss eventually came back to our area to finalize the business matter with the okra farmer that day. One thing I remember before the boss arrived to finalize that sale—he had a big smile on his chubby face as he was walking towards us, and he was talking with everyone he passed by before he arrived at our area. I am sure he was happy because he probably won that load of money on the table, because I remember one day when he did not win.

The boss came back from gambling one day, and he was in an unbelievably bad mood; he'd probably lost a lot of money gambling that day. He started complaining and fussing and told me to hand over the daily intake of money. He counted it, gave me my ten dollars for my day's work, told me to go home and that he would not need me anymore. He fired me for no reason. Let me reword that politically correctly. He "released" me from my services and responsibilities.

I went home, told my mom, and she did not know what to think of it either. I reassured her I did nothing to get fired. Now, again, this is the summertime; there's no school. So, two days went by with my not going to work, but the phone rang early, about 7:00 a.m., on the third morning; it was my boss asking my mom why I had not shown up for work the last two days.

The two of them had a conversation, and I heard my mom loudly say, *"My son would not lie to me; he said you fired him for no reason."*

After my mom finished expressing her thoughts and opinions, my boss finally admitted he was wrong and begged my mom to let me return to work. My mom said okay.

I returned to work in the French Market. I loved it—the people, the place, the sounds, and Oh, the money was good too.

Here in chapter seven, I tried to highlight those stories I thought were important and relevant to my social assimilation while living on Law Street. There are many more stories I could have shared; actually, Law Street could be its own book. In the next chapter, I will share with you some of my experiences from my freshman year of high school while still living on Law Street.

Chapter VIII

Freshman Year—High School

"Soul Power"

R & B singer James Brown had a 1974 song titled "Soul Power." If I could sum up starting high school, it would be…soul power.

My freshman year of high school, in the fall of 1972, I attended Redemptorist Catholic High School in the Irish Channel. I was one of the first twelve Black students to attend this school in the old Uptown neighborhood. As a small kid, I wanted to attend Saint Aloysius Catholic High School, Mr. Tom Benson's high school; he was the owner of the New Orleans Saints. Saint Aloysius was located on the corner of Esplanade Avenue and North Rampart Street, but the school closed and merged with Cor Jesu Catholic High School, which was located on Elysian Fields Avenue in Gentilly. The merger of those two schools produced Brother Martin Catholic High School in 1969.

As a kid, my mom would regularly drive pass Saint Aloysius on our visits to the French Market, and I would see all the students. Though they were all White, as a little kid, I still hoped I could attend high school there one day. Sometimes when we would drive by, the football team would be street-level practicing right behind the school on a small, grassy open lot. I could see on the red-and-white football helmets a crusader mascot mounted on a horse. I imagined that crusader going to war, and as a young kid, that was the coolest thing on a football helmet.

In hindsight, I probably would not have attended Saint Aloysius when I became of age to attend high school, because my social and instinctive experiences would change very significantly.

My mom's desire was for me to attend Saint Augustine, the all-boys, all-Black Catholic high school, and for some strange reason, I was never thoroughly convinced that Saint Aug was the school for me. I was never mesmerized by the school colors or its mascot. A purple knight? What the hell is or was that? Are they, the students, purple people eaters? Saint Aug's mascot was not a powerful image, like a crusader or a ram; it was just a purple person dressed as a knight. Sorry, I liked the school's band and the football team, particularly King Solomon, but I could not see myself as a purple knight. Therefore, I never pleaded to attend school there.

On top of that, it was an all-boy Catholic high school. Going to school without girls was definitely out of the question because I had already become acquainted with the birds and the bees at a very earlier age. I was a fourteen-year-old handsome kid with a trendy Afro hairstyle. During the seventies, Afros were appealing, and meeting charming, attractive girls was never a problem for me.

I persuaded Mom to let me attend this coed Catholic high school, Redemptorist, because, as I've said, attending any school without girls was out of the question. I enrolled, school started, and only one thing was missing—there were no Black girls attending Redemptorist…none! And in 1972, the interracial dating scene was not as common as it is now, not in New Orleans, and especially not in uptown, blue-collar Irish Channel/New Orleans.

There were only twelve Black male students in a school of over 400 students, and half of the Black guys played sports.

We had some White friends in school, but they were only "school" friends; outside of school functions, we did not mingle or socialize with White students, nor did the White students socialize with us. In high school, my White friends (or were they really friends?) never invited us to parties, picnics, or social functions. That is the way it was in New Orleans, based on my experience with race relations in the seventies, other than the king-cake parties in grammar school.

Based on what little integration there was in New Orleans schools, businesses, and politics, we New Orleanians were encouraged to socialize "only" within our own culture. When considering Mardi Gras clubs, Mardi Gras parade organizations, or private social clubs, from my viewpoint, there was no integration, not yet, before the eighties.

Redemptorist High School and Gymnasium in the Irish Channel, at Saint Mary and Annunciation Streets.

I was a freshman in the fall of '72, and I tried out for the JV basketball team that fall. I made it through the last week of cuts, but I was not eligible to play in any games if I made the team because I lived out of the district. Therefore, I had to sit out one year. I was one of the top players at the guard position, but there was a problem. All the White guys knew I was good, and my relationship with them went downhill every time I had a good practice session. I probably would have made the varsity team too that fall, but I sustained a hand injury that was agonizing.

The fingernail on my right thumb was halfway torn back, and it aggravated me so badly during practice that one day I literally ripped the entire fingernail off. Then, after ripping the nail off, every time I bounced, shot, or rebounded the basketball, the pain was severe, and the injury was not healing fast enough. I asked the coach could I sit out some practice drills until my thumb healed, and he told me yes. He informed me he could not save a spot for me on the team because players' performances during practice would determine team placement.

He also informed me there were two more weeks of tryouts. I still could perform in other physical activities related to training and game preparation—running, exercise, lifting weights, etc. I just could not do anything that involved controlling the ball or physical contact with my finger. Unfortunately for me, I could not take the pain during tryout practices anymore, so I quit.

The coach did not ask or encourage me to remain on the team. The coach, knowing I was one of the better players, did not even assist me at any time with my finger injury or suggested what I should do to help it heal faster.

Some White guys on the team approached me in the locker room on the day I quit and said they had just heard the news or good news. I confirmed their insecure curiosities. Several guys seemed to be extremely happy and basically started talking about who would or would not make the team.

At that point, I was getting closer to…"Soul Power."

Mark Essex

Now, that I did not participate in basketball for the fall of '72 and early spring of '73. I decided to try out for the football team during a very early spring practice.

While participating and trying out for football during a very cold January in 1973, a strange thing happened in the New Orleans community. A sniper by the name of Mark Essex stormed into a Howard Johnson's motel with a rifle in his hand and had a private race war on his mind.

He spent the rest of the day shooting people from the roof of the hotel. He killed two hotel workers, three cops, and a newlywed couple; he wounded twenty-six others. Eventually, he was shot down by Marine sharpshooters who were called in to take him out.

I had to ride the transit bus early every morning to get to Redemptorist by 6:45 a.m., when classes started. I woke up early, 5:30 a.m., dressed, ate, and took off for school. On Monday, January 8, 1973, I was not sure if the transit system was running. So off to school I went on the day of the Mark Essex incident.

My mom was a rock-solid believer in perfect school attendance. We dared not miss a day of school, and she would not let us stay home from school unless we were dying or could not walk. In our house, you better not pretend or fake a sickness just to stay home from school. My mom would examine us as if she were a doctor, and that examination itself was enough for us to say we were not sick enough to stay home. If we had a runny nose, cough, or fever, that was not sick enough to stay home. Therefore, staying home just because someone was shooting off the top of a building at police was not enough to stay home from school either. The administrators of the school should have just called school off that day because every class I attended had the TV on, and all we did that day was watch the sniper report.

Spring football was in full swing, so after watching the sniper report all day, we had football practice. I had worked my way up to second string team member at corner back and wide receiver. I would have been the second-string corner back and on special teams as a sophomore that coming fall '73, but things really took a change for me physically that January 1973.

Scarlet Fever

Yes, Mark Essex was shooting at policemen, in January of '73, and several days later, right after Mark Essex's shoot-out, something shot into my blood system that almost killed me. I was exceptionally sick one day and literally could not walk; my mom and I did not think it was the flu. I repeatedly, for several years, suffered from swelling of the gums around my back molars that had silver cavity fillings. That probably happened because of terrible dental work when I was seven years old. The fillings were not done correctly; therefore, food residue would settle deep in my molars and infection would occur.

During past sicknesses or when my gums would swell up, my mom would doctor on me with her prescriptions of penicillin or other antibiotics, and the swelling would always go away. Therefore, on this day when I started feeling extremely sick, around the last week of January, 1973, my mom assumed taking penicillin again would kill off the sickness. It did not, and the fever and sore throat intensified. I could barely walk, so for the very first time in my life, I fulfilled the only requirement for staying home from school. I was about to die.

After staying home for two days, the sickness worsened, and a round, pink-red, bubbly, blistering rash started developing all over my body, from the neck down. At that point, my mom knew this was something more than just fever and swollen gums around my molars, so she took me to Charity Hospital. My mom had a political lawyer friend who was socially connected at the time; therefore, instead of going to the emergency room and waiting, we entered the front door of Charity Hospital and went straight to the administrator's office because my mom's friend knew the hospital's director.

The director of Charity Hospital came out of his office, looked over my skin thoroughly, and then he summoned the head doctor of the Dermatology Department, Dr. Wilder. The Doctor looked at the red-pink blisters on my hands and arms for about five seconds, and he immediately said I needed to be admitted into the hospital. What I had would not heal at home without proper medication and medical care. According to the doctor, the penicillin did not kill off the bacteria in my body, and somehow I had contracted scarlet fever.

My entire body, from the neck down, was covered in the rash. It was not a dry rash, but a warm, wet, big-bubble rash, and it constantly itched. I wasn't allowed to scratch—NO SCRATCHING—or I would rupture the blisters and make scars all over my body. Oh, how miserable!

At Charity Hospital, the administration cleared out an entire ward of people, twelve beds, and I was housed on the seventh floor. I was the only patient and had the entire ward to myself. I could now begin my personal time of suffering. For three to four nights, I could not sleep and could not scratch my hot, itching body. You have no idea what pain and suffering that fourteen-year-old boy went through those first three nights before the medication took effect.

While not being able to sleep because of the intense itching and pain, I would just walk, and walk, and walk, up and down the ward, walking in a circle, walking in the hallway, sitting in the telephone booth in the hall a little while, then walking again, all night until I became so weary and had to lie down from fatigue. The itching was so intense that I could not keep still, and because I could not scratch, the itching seemed more severe. Because of the acute pain and high fever, I could not have any visitors—NONE. No family members or friends visited me the first week.

I remember the first two nights during my "walking dead" routine. I called my mom from the telephone booth at about midnight, crying and telling her how bad my skin burned and itched and that I could not scratch, nor could I sleep. She just cried on the other end of the phone and tried to encourage me to stay strong.

After about six days, I was starting to feel better. The fever and the itching were less intense, but I still had this ugly rash all over my body. One day, the nurse in my ward called me up to the desk to take a phone call, and it was my mom. She was on her way to visit me, so she asked if I would like her to bring me something special.

That was one of the best things I'd ever heard because that hospital food was horrendous. My response was *"YES!!!!! Bring me a good ole fried-oyster po'boy sandwich, not dressed, just butter, pickles, and ketchup on French bread."* I also asked for an order of French fries and a Barq's root beer. Barq's was a locally-owned manufacturer of bottled sodas in New Orleans; it went out of business in the late nineties.

Success, love and
Best wishes to

DIANE
GALATAS

from

your brother Herman
Galatas and grandfather
Sidney Moore

Me and my sister, Charity Hospital, spring of 1973.

As the healing progressed, my sister visited me a couple of times, and my mom took the above picture of her and me one day. In the Saint Mary Academy Catholic High School yearbook, 1972-1973, you can still see that picture in the back Salutations section.

Some of my close personal friends, guys and girls, visited me while I was in the hospital. They came as a group, about ten of them. We had a good time that one evening. On another occasion, I remember my two "girlfriends" I had been dating; they both visited me "accidentally" at the same time. *Awkward! Not good, playa…not good!!*

The three of us tried to hold a diplomatic conversation; that seem to go nowhere until one of them decided to leave. What I remember after that visit was one of the older gentlemen, who was in the ward across from me, advised me on which one I should keep dating. Understandably, his eyes were on the prettier one.

My healing continued, and I gained my physical strength back and returned to normal living after two weeks in Charity, but I still had this ugly dry rash all over my body.

During the winter time, it hardly ever snows in New Orleans, maybe every twenty years, but on the day I was released in early February of 1973, it was sleeting heavily, mixed with a little snow, in our neighborhood, but not enough snow throughout New Orleans for major news coverage.

My sister did not know I was being released earlier that morning. So, my mom asked my stepdad to take me to pick up Dianne after school to surprise her. He decided not to drive all the way to Saint Mary's Academy in the sleet, so both of us just waited in the car on the corner of Franklin Avenue and Gentilly Boulevard for Dianne to get off the Chef Menteur bus, to board the Franklin Avenue bus.

When that transit bus she was on finally arrived, Dianne stepped off, and my stepdad drove up next to her while she and a friend were walking. When she looked in the car and saw me, she started screaming in celebration. I opened the door, got out, and we jumped around in the sleet for a minute, laughing; then we hopped back into the car and drove home.

Speech Contest, Me?

I went back to school at Redemptorist bravely, and students could see the remnants of the ugly rash. My skin was peeling, and there was a sort of discoloration in my skin, light and dark spots that would eventually go away. Everyone in school avoided me as if I had the bubonic plague, and even some of my closest Black friends teased me and told me not to get too close to them because I had "the germ." Do you know what it feels like to be ostracized by an entire school body? Think about it.

Neither the doctor nor my parents would have allowed me to go back to school if the authorities had not approved it, but teens…let's just say, their world is mindless. I cannot blame them. I was a silly teen myself, and teens, especially those in the seventies, had their distorted, warped way of understanding reality.

My skin started clearing up over time, and while attending Redemptorist that late spring, the English department announced a speech contest. There would be tryouts for anyone in the school interested in representing their class in each category—poetry, drama, short readings, etc. Each grade level would hold tryouts, and the two winners from each category would represent their class. The main event, when all classes would compete against each other, would be on a weekday night two weeks after tryouts.

During the beginning of English class one day, when the speech contest was announced, some crazy feeling came over me and moved me to try out for the poetry-reading section. Before I informed the teacher that I wanted to try out, I turned around and picked this book of poems off the classroom bookshelf. I looked in it and saw this poem. It was easy to read, so I figured it would be a walk in the park.

I approached my English teacher, who was a genuinely nice lady, and informed her that I wanted to try out for the poetry-reading section of the contest. She was happily surprised and encouraged me to participate.

Now I was scared. *What the hell did I just do?*

She asked if I had a selection, and I said yes. She then asked what it was, and when I told her, she said, *"Excellent choice!!"*

I selected to read Edgar Allan Poe's poem "Annabel Lee." Do not ask me why. I do not know why, but I just did it. I did not even know who the hell Edgar Allan Poe was.

With that poem, I participated in the preliminary round for selecting two ninth graders to represent the freshman class in the poetry section of the speech contest. To my and my teacher's surprise, the tryouts, particularly my tryout, went extremely well.

The poem reads:

It was many and many a year ago,
In a kingdom by the sea,
That a maiden there lived whom you may know
By the name of Annabel Lee;
And this maiden she lived with no other thought
Than to be loved and loved by me.

I was a child, and she was a child
In this kingdom by the sea,
But we loved with a love that was more than love,
I and my Annabel Lee,
With a love that the winged seraphs of heaven
Coveted her and me.

And this was the reason that, long ago,
In this kingdom by the sea,
A wind blew out of a cloud
Chilling my Annabel Lee;
So that her king born kinsman came
And bore her away from me,
To shut her up in a sepulcher

In this kingdom by the sea.

The angels, not half so happy in Heaven,
Went envying her and me.
Yes! That was the reason as all men know,
In this kingdom by the sea,
That the wind came out of a cloud by night,
Chilling and killing my Annabel Lee.

But our love it was stronger by far than the love
Of those who were older than we,
Of many far wiser than we,
And neither the angels in Heaven above,
Nor the demons down under the sea,
Can ever dissever my soul from the soul
Of the beautiful Annabel Lee.

For the moon never beams without bringing me dreams,
Of the beautiful Annabel Lee;
And the stars never rise but I see the bright eyes
Of the beautiful Annabel Lee;
And so, all the night-tide, I lie down by the side
Of my darling, my darling, my life and my bride,
In her sepulcher there by the sea,
In her tomb by the sounding of the sea.

—Edgar Allan Poe

I read that poem for tryouts during English class that day, and the entire class voted for me and another skinny, brunette White girl to represent the ninth-grade class for the poetry reading contest.

When I arrived home that day after school, I told my mom, and she was happy and excited. She told my sister to work with me every night until the event, which she did. Everything was going well, and then the night arrived for the contest.

It was time for the big show, and I was extremely nervous. *Why did I get involved with this?* My family, the four of us, drove to my school that evening. We arrived and then proceeded to a room where all the poetry-reading participants from all classes were going to compete. The hallway of the school was packed, and it seemed as if every person who was going to perform that night, their families, and closest friends were there.

My family found nice seats in the room where the contest would take place and sat there, waiting for the contest to begin. I could tell Dianne was a little uncomfortable in the all-White setting because she had never been in an integrated school environment, never. Remember, I was the integration child, so I had been attending school with White kids since the sixth grade in the fall of 1969.

The buzz in the hallway and in that room among my school acquaintances and their parents was that I was the best contestant in the poetic-reading category; I was favored to win the contest. Imagine that, in 1973, at an all-White school, the White kids are saying, to win, you need to perform better than the Black student.

My math teacher, a charming, older White nun, overheard the buzz about me, so she came into the room to hear me when it was my turn to recite. She wanted to hear one of her best math students compete as the front-runner in the poetry-reading contest.

The rules for each recitation were:

1. The poem had to be at least one minute, but not more than three minutes.

2. Pronunciation had to be perfect.

3. Contestants had to have good posture while reading.

4. Contestants had to make eye contact with the audience while reading.

We, the freshman-class representatives, practiced our poems in every English class, every day before the main night. My poem was just a little bit under a minute; my English teacher knew that, and she said it was okay because she had coached us regarding the other skills on which we would be judged–posture, eye contact, etc.—and she said those skills were perfect. I knew I had to perform perfectly, meaning I had to take my time, articulate every word correctly, not make a mistake, and make sure I looked at the audience while performing the poem. I practiced and practiced and practiced before that event, to the point that it was perfect.

In the room that night, there was only one judge evaluating our performance. She was an older, heavyset White nun.

Thank you, Jesus, I am safe.

The contest started, and the two representatives from each grade level competing were called up to read in alphabetical order by last name. The little White, skinny girl in my English class read her poem before me. She was horrible. She missed the pronunciation of several words and had to go back one time to the beginning of a stanza in her poem. She was so nervous that it caused her to shake anxiously the entire time. She was shaking so much I thought her skinny knees were going to shatter.

Another upper classman, a junior White girl, went before me too. She had this big, big, big book opened in front of her, and she could barely hold it up. She kept her head down in the book, did not make eye contact with the audience, and you really could not hear everything or understand what she was reading half the time. Then my time came.

I went up, took a deep breath, and sounded off. Word after word, head up the entire time, smiling, I never looked down at the poem in the book. I had memorized it; hence, I gazed at the audience the entire time left to right, right to left. I made eye contact, and I stood like a statue, smiling and making eye contact with the audience—picture-perfect!!! I shocked myself. When I finished, I received the loudest ovation and longest applause of all the contestants.

The competitions in the other rooms ended, too, as we made our way to the gym for the announcement of winners for all categories. While walking with the parents and students from the other rooms reserved for the drama and short-story readings competitions. We were asked what was the reason or purpose for that loud ovation they had heard coming from our room.

As we entered the gym, my math teacher came over to hang out with my parents, and she was more elated than we were. She just kept talking and talking about my performance and how perfect it was and how proud of me she was. She told my family that not only was my performance good that night, but also I was one of her best math students.

The judges for all categories were evaluating their results, and the gym was filling up with parents and spectators. Based on what I saw that night, it appeared that the students had started supporting the Black student who almost died of scarlet fever—not because he almost died, but because he was a human being, a good student, and the best poem reader. Contestants that I had competed against came up to me and told me how well I had done and wished me well; many contestants' parents from the poetry-reading room wished me good luck too.

I could not believe several of the kids and their parents were congratulating me; I had not even won yet. They'd probably heard that I was the kid who'd almost died. Some of them had observed for themselves that this little Black/ Creole boy, who had "the germ" and almost died, competed in a poem-reading speech contest. This was the same kid that the entire school—administrators, staff, and student body— avoided for several weeks after he returned to school, and now his performance was better than what they expected.

We, my parents, the students, their parents, and all the other spectators—were "integrating" during that one moment in time in the gym that night as we were waiting for the results. We were all literally treating each other as equals, just as the people in Miami, Florida, did when they jumped into the pool to save my sister, or the nurses with yellow hair did when they filled my pockets with candy every time I left the doctor's office.

The time had arrived. I felt as if I were on the basket-ball court playing against all the big guys and beating the pants off them. I was ready to call out, "Who's got next," because I knew I was about to hit the big three-point shot at the buzzer and win the game.

The announcements came, and winners in other categories went up on the stage to get their trophies for first, second, and third place. Those winners had big smiles on their faces. Our category came up; my heart was beating fast.

The announcer said, *"For poetry reading, third place goes to…"* The skinny girl from my freshman class whose knees were knocking when she read her poem.

Okay, good. I know I got first place now.

"Second place goes to…" Some other sophomore student, a guy who was in our contest. Without question I was better than him too, just based on the applause I received.

Now… *"First place in the poetry-reading contest goes to…"*

NOT ME!!!!!

Rather, the junior girl who had her head down in the book while she read her poem extremely quietly; she never even made eye contact with the audience.

WHAT THE HELL JUST HAPPENED!!!???

I could not believe it, and neither could any other person who had been in our room. The contest's family members and friends who were in our room during my reading made a loud negative vocal outburst—the only way I can describe it is *"AAWWW!!!"* and it was very loud.

My math teacher, bless her heart, reacted hysterically. She lost her scruples; I thought the lady was going to have a heart attack. I had never witness this old nun lose her cool, ever. She was furious and angrier than any of my family members.

My family members and I, we just looked at each other and took a deep breath because, deep down inside our hearts and in our minds, we knew what just happened—"White preference." So we turned around and started heading out of the gym.

My math teacher ran behind us, and she begged us not to leave until she spoke with the judge, so she could provide us with a reasonable explanation as to why I did not win. My mom decided to be respectful of my math teacher's request and waited.

While we were standing at the gym door, waiting to exit, several of the parents of students from our contest category approached us and apologized on the behalf of the judge. Those parents, they also knew what just happened too, and I truly believe the sincerity of their apologies were genuine.

The junior student girl who'd won, her boyfriend, and her parents came over and talked with us for several minutes, trying to console me and my parents. They were shocked because the girl, the winner, admitted to us that she did not deserve to win. This young lady said her classmates in her English class had voted for the two worst poetry readers to represent their junior class. Why? As a practical joke.

Finally, my math teacher made it back to us; the judge had told her I did not meet the one-minute-minimum reading time. So, we asked what the time was. My math teacher replied that the judge stated my reading time registered at fifty-eight seconds. The math teacher also informed us that the judge proclaimed I had rhymed too much—repeat, I rhymed too much—during a poetry reading of a rhyming poem. The poem is written as a rhyme, but I rhymed too much. Lady, Nun, Ma'am, I did not write the poem, but yet you condemned me for a rhyming poem written by Edgar Allan Poe. That is similar to saying I have too many ones in a one-plus-one math formula that equals two. In her opinion, one plus one does not equal two.

That night, I knew the real meaning of James Brown's song "Soul Power."

I enrolled at Redemptorist as an open-minded, innocent, young Black kid trying to embrace civility. Hoping to live the "I Have a Dream" lifestyle, being respectful, treating others the way I wanted to be treated, being kind, and helping make this a better world to live in.

And what did I get out of attending Redemptorist? I got… "Soul Power." That experience and some others that happened later that spring of '73 while attending that all-White school caused me to grow up socially amazingly fast and initiated my embracing of "political Blackness." So now I knew and understood "Soul Power" at age fifteen. Losing that speech contest and my not being awarded the MVP of male sports at Our Lady Star of the Sea School confirmed my social aware-ness of racial discrimination.

Attacked by White King Kong

There were many racially tense situations while I attended Redemptorist, and sometimes I just overlooked the jokes and the belittlement because it was not directed specifically at me. With the end of spring approaching and the weather getting warmer, it did not help the racial tensions. One day during third period, the boys' PE period was a combined PE class of all grade levels. Athletes were scheduled to run around the gym and lift weights during PE.

A heated conversation started developing between one of the football coaches and a running back on the school's football team. This student who was a senior and would eventually graduate later that spring, was jogging around the gym's basketball court. Every time he passed by the coach, he would say something, and the coach would respond. I did not hear all the details, but it had something to do with my *"big Afro."*

I remember the coach saying to that student, *"Just leave it alone, Frank; we will handle it."* Meaning, he, the coach, would handle my hair issue.

The rule for hair length for boys at the school was that hair could not be below the bottom of the ear; if so, you had to get it cut just to that point. The way I got around that hair rule was that my Afro went up; therefore, it was not below the bottom of my ear. Now remember, this is 1972-73, the long-hair, big-Afro era, the Jackson 5, Led Zeppelin, the Rolling Stones. Long hair is the style of the era. The picture of me and my sister, earlier in this chapter show my afro. Note: The camera flash caused a shadow in the ground, making the afro look larger than it actually was.

This one senior football player was upset that I could have an Afro that went up, and in his eyes, my hair was too big. But the Afro was not lower than the bottom of my ear; thus, I complied with the hair rule. So, I did not get a haircut all year. This really annoyed this senior football player, and not just that guy, but several other students who were afraid to express themselves to the coaches, but would make comments to me. Therefore, as this one complaining senior continued to jog around the gym floor and lash out with his outrageous comments about my hair, I overheard one of his insulting comments while I was over on the other side of the gym in the weight station, lifting weights.

Let me set the tone. I was only about five eight, 120, pounds, and this guy, the starting running back on the football team, was a graduating senior, about six two, 200 pounds, all muscles, big as a gorilla. He was not a bully, and I had never had a run-in with him before. I concluded, since he was graduating, he figured he could speak up for the other guys who were upset about my big Afro too. For those guys, seeing this Black kid every day with this big Afro was really starting to make them angry because I was into style, and they were not. And to add fire to the situation, some of the girls thought I was cute and looked like the Jackson 5, and they, the boys, could not handle that.

This football player, still jogging in a circle around the gym floor, continued to shout out insults nonstop. I overheard something that was derogatory about Black people, something along the lines of *"a hairy monkey and now he,"* meaning me, not following the school's hair rules. Just then, he stopped running and stood in front of the coach, mouthing off insistently and brashly. I could hear their entire conversation at the other end of the gym. His verbal hostility amplified, lashing out at all Black citizens for no reason.

I heard another insulting statement about Black people; that is when I reacted, and my "Soul Power" stirred up in me. From the far corner of the gym, I screamed something very offensive back at him. Why did I do that?

At that moment, this student responded so angrily and started running violently towards me with every bit of energy in his body thrusting him forward. I just stood there, not knowing what to do as he charged toward me. I saw anger and hatred on his face as he got closer. Then I got a little scared, but before I could make a getaway, he tackled my little five eight, 120-pound, fragile frame. He picked me up just as King Kong does the damsel in the movie, and he threw me down on the weight bench. I am lying there on my back as he grabs both of my shoulders; he is now shaking me up and down on that weight bench while screaming how he is going to kick my ass.

While in this physically uncontrollable fit of verbal outrage against Black people, he verbally abused me and the entire Black population while shaking the hell out of me. I tried to fight him off, which I could not do, so I tried to keep my cool until it took three coaches and about five students to pull him off me. The coaches had to drag him away by his two arms because he would not stop trying to attack me, and as they were dragging him away, he was still making derogatory insults about Black people. I just stood there in shock.

No one, not one, said anything to me as I stood there. No one, not even a coach, asked me if he injured me. I knew my place in that school, on that day. The coaches then instructed all of us students to hit the locker room to change.

There were several students in that gym class who I thought were my friends, but to my surprise, they all backed this student one hundred percent as we were changing back into our uniforms. And even right after that incident, right there in the locker room, several students were directing insulting statements at me. I felt as if I had just committed the worst crime in history.

That day, I knew what loneliness feels like, and maybe I did have "the germ." So, after that encounter, I avoided contact with all White students until the end of the year. I learned that day about racial disparities and racial differences. I just sat there in fear of my life.

None of those students thought the senior's actions were wrong, except the Black students once the story surfaced all thorugh-out the school. One guy even had the audacity to say, *"If you would have gotten your hair cut short, none of this would have happened."*

Really...? Hair...? Is that what this is all about...an Afro? Just a year ago, I had a "Black" cop tell me to get a haircut because I looked like a girl, and now I have White students furious over my hair style too. How can my hair hurt you? How? Oh my God!!!

During that school year, not one coach or administrator told me to get a haircut. None. So, did I do something wrong? No. Those guys were jealous and fearful of my big Afro. Yes, I had "Soul Power," and I was not going to deny it.

I did not have one White friend that day. I think I experienced, but not on a major scale, what Black individuals went through trying to cross the bridge in Selma, Alabama during the early Civil Rights Movement. They wanted the right to vote; I wanted the right to wear an Afro.

Looking back now, it was not okay for that White student to make derogatory statements about Black people, and it was not all right that nothing was done. That senior football player broke a major school rule that day by violently fighting and trying to kill someone, but he did not get suspended or expelled; he ended up graduating without apologizing to me.

The coaches said I provoked him when I shouted an insulting statement back at him from across the gym; they believed, if I had not screamed out to him, they had everything under control. Then, the coach said we both should had been suspended, but because we both were wrong, they let it go.

Here is what the coaches had under control: a White student using derogatory words, portraying Black people as ignorant monkeys, and violently attacking a Black student. Those actions did not get the White student suspended from a predominantly-White Catholic high school in New Orleans's Irish Channel neighborhood in 1973. OKAY. Y'all coaches had it under control.

I now had another dose of "Soul Power." I may not have been out on the streets protesting for the right to eat at the lunch counters or sit in the front of the bus, or protesting in Selma, Alabama, for the right to vote. But I absolutely was not going to let a high schooler that was my equivalent and those coaches get away with my hearing them and accepting insulting remarks about Black people. They, the coaches, never corrected the kid, not one time. I had already had the speech contest stolen from me because of my race, and in the preceding chapter I had the MVP sports award stolen from me in eighth grade because of my race.

Yes, I called them out; it was time for me to start taking a stand for what was right. I did not need Big Dee to fight for me anymore.

Who Said That? That Is a No-No!

My mom came to pick me up after school one late spring day after that gym incident. I would usually ride the transit bus home from school, but this day my mom decided to pick me up. I was standing out in front of school when she pulled up in the car.

When I got in, she said, *"Did cha hear dat?"*

I said, *"Yes."*

She said, *"What cha do bout dat?"*

I told her, *"Mom, every day I heard dat, all day, all da time."*

Somebody screamed the N-word at us. Whoever screamed those words directed it at the wrong person that day. I looked around to see who said that, and there was only one guy walking pass us. I do not know exactly who said it; it could have been said by someone on the second story, out of the window, or someone around the corner, or across the street, but somebody was about to take the fall for it.

My mom jumped out of the car, and we went into the principal's office. I followed her into the building, and I saw my mom verbally delivering all her frustrations about the school. My mom gave the principal a piece of her mind. You really do not want me to repeat what she told this nun. Because of the verbal belittlement and harassment while picking me up and her own dissatisfactions about what happened on the night of the speech contest, the principal received a full verbal assault. God, please forgive my mom. But after being called the N-word, my mom had to get it off her chest.

After my mom calmed down, the principal asked if I knew who blurted that racial slur. I told the principal the name of the student I saw passing by at the time. Unfortunately for him, he was walking by, so he got fingered. I have no idea who actually said it. But how many times have Black individuals been accused of something they didn't do?

That poor guy had to call my mom and apologize, and he apologized to me at school too. But he kept repeating while apologizing that he did not say that. This kid just happened to be the scapegoat that day. Poor kid. I really felt bad about it, but things happen. Sorry, dude.

As the spring of '73 ended and the summer began, summer practice sessions at Redemptorist High School for basketball and football started. I had determined and prepared myself mentally to return to Redemptorist, I was projected to start on the varsity basketball team in the fall of '73, the next school year as a sophomore, based on my performance during that summer. As for football, I was placed on the second team backup as a corner back.

All the football players had to attend weightlifting and football walk-through play practice three times a week during the summer. I attended those summer practice sessions for football until it was time to go to football camp.

A couple of days before football camp, while standing on the sidelines with helmets on, walking through football plays, one student screamed to a coach, *"Is he gonna get a haircut too?"* Before that, no coach had told me I had too much hair sticking out of the bottom of the football helmet.

Basically, I got tired of hearing that I needed a haircut. I was not going to get rid of my Afro; therefore, going back to Redemptorist High School was not an option anymore, I was tired of being ridiculed for no other reason than my hair. I now had "Soul Power," and I was not going to lose my "Soul Power" for those Irish Channel people.

What is disturbing is that I liked Redemptorist High School. I liked the mascot, the ram. I loved riding the city bus route uptown to the Irish Channel, with all of the pretty Xavier Prep High School girls. I loved the school uniforms and colors. I even painted my room at home with the school colors. One side of my room was yellow, and the other side was blue. I loved the image of the ram's horns on the helmets. I loved my big book bag, yellow and blue; it had a ram on it too.

The White guys who tossed sticks, bottles, and stones at my friend and me on top of the Franklin Avenue Bridge, and those students and coaches at Redemptorist High School,"educated" me in racial differences. I learned from them to be intolerant, not from any of my beautiful family members.

As an adult, it has taken me years to repress discriminatory ideology, and at times it has been extremely hard, without question. How can a person not have racial convictions when you are attacked for no reason other than your skin color or your hair?

Chapter IX

Spring and Summer of 1973

My New Friends

While still living on Law Street during the late spring and summer of '73, my social interests progressed; consequently, my attention was elsewhere, other than on returning to Redemptorist High School to play football and basketball in the fall of 1973. My new interest was music and in particular, R & B. I did not play my trumpet in Redemptorist's school band during ninth grade. I just played and practiced on my own at home, trying to replicate what I heard on the radio or on my home "vinyl record player."

We all know New Orleans is the birthplace of jazz and specifically Dixieland jazz, but in my social circle of friends, we were not playing any form of jazz during the seventies. We played what we heard on the R&B radio stations, WBOK and WYLD. Not just my circle of friends, but many other teens and adults in New Orleans were playing and dancing to what we heard on the radio. As for Jazz? Forget that stuff, which I now regret.

In New Orleans during the spring and summer of '73, there seemed to be a local R&B band practicing in every neighborhood, every day. If you rode your bike through different neighborhoods, especially in the Village, you would hear several R&B bands practicing in different homes. Some of the popular bands of that era were the Meters, Chocolate Milk, Stop Inc., Trac One, The Del Rays, The Soul Sensations, Louisiana Purchase, and Better Half. These bands and numerous other bands performed during high school events, dances, proms, etc., and for wedding, parties, and other social events.

While attending Redemptorist from 1972 to 1973, I started spending a lot of time in a neighborhood that was located on the north side of the Ninth Ward, Pontchartrain Park, or as we referred to it, the Park. Countless middle-class Black families lived in the Park; there were Black school administrators, teachers, postal workers, Black nurses, and doctors, etc., and eventually, New Orleans's first Black mayor, Ernest Dutch Morial. He lived right on Press Drive, across the street from the Pontchartrain Park playground. The Park is also the neighborhood where Southern University at New Orleans is located.

I lived about three miles from the Park. Therefore, I would ride my bike from our Law Street home on the weekends and hang out all day in the Park.

Meeting My Best Friends for the First Time

One early spring day right after my scarlet-fever sickness, I started discussing with a friend of mine, who lived in the Park, about starting an R&B band. He said he had crossed paths and connected with two guys on the local bus one day; they were backup musicians for a Black gospel vocal group. One guy played the lead guitar, and the other guy was a bass guitarist. After that talk, he decided to contact these two musicians about starting a band. That would be the start of a long friendship with Ted and Ricky.

Yes, we started a small R&B band, and we had more house rehearsals or jam sessions than we played in public. We were home musicians.

Ted was one of the best Black lead guitarists in the city during that period. He was so gifted that several years later he would eventually end up playing for an all-White rock band that performed in Fat City, which was a nightclub area in Metairie, Louisiana. Imagine that in the seventies—the only soul brother in a rock band, on lead guitar. Now, that's a story.

Ricky played bass guitar, and he lived about a mile from my home. Ted lived "down in the Parish," as it was referred to, which meant Ted lived in Saint Bernard Parish, in a small town called Arabi, in the southeast portion of the Lower Ninth Ward. Ted's house was a good distance from where Ricky and I lived in the Upper Ninth Ward.

Ricky and Ted were my age, fifteen years old, and they were backup musicians for this all-male, Black, vocal gospel group that I we referred to as the Big Brothers. All four were middle-aged gentlemen, thirty-five to forty years old, and all weighed over 200 pounds. The Big Brothers would travel throughout the New Orleans metropolitan area to perform in Black Baptist churches on Sundays. Many times, I traveled alongside Ricky and Ted as they went to perform as backup musicians for the Big Brothers.

Ted, Ricky, and I became remarkably close, to the point that this Creole, light complexion Catholic boy was hanging out in Black Baptist churches throughout the city; truth be told, that was not common back in the seventies. I know it's hard to believe and understand, but facts are facts. Most Creole, people were Catholics, and most Black Baptist and Creole people did not meet on Sunday morning for fellowship—sad but true.

Because of my upbringing, being the only light-complexion person while I attended the Big Brothers' performances never overwhelmed me. To me, people were people, and because once again, my family members were both light- and dark- complexion.

As I occasionally traveled with Ted, Ricky, and the Big Brothers, the Big Brothers thought that I was starting to influence Ted and Ricky with my "social ethics" and that I was steering Ted and Ricky away from playing and performing gospel music. Well, truthfully, I was.

They, the Big Brothers, probably called me the devil, but the fact of the matter was that Ted and Ricky wanted to experience life and all its opportunities, rather than just attend gospel rehearsals and performances. Ted and Ricky had their own unique personalities, and they were listening to what was being played on the radio too, and funk music was starting to peak.

You honestly think this one Creole kid had a major influence on what type of music two talented teenage musicians wanted to play? Get a life, Big Brothers!!!!

Times A-Changing

My friendship with Ted and Ricky helped them to transition into a social circle of people to whom they were not accustomed. One night, some friends from the Park informed me about a dance party at the Autocrat Club. Now, trust me when I tell you this: The Autocrat Club was known as the "brown-paper-bag club" that started way before my time.

Oh, you don't know what I mean when I say "brown-paper-bag club"?

I explained that back in chapter two. Men could only be members of this club if their skin complexion was lighter than a brown paper bag. Not literally, that was the common joke; however, the majority of the members were indeed Creoles.

The Autocrat Club, on Saint Bernard Avenue, New Orleans, Louisiana.

On a Friday night, the daughter of one of the senior members of the club was giving a dance party. Back then, you did not need an invitation to attend; you just crashed the party. On the night of this party, I invited Ted and Ricky to join me at a party being given by Creole Black people. They agreed to come along, and they were glad they did.

No! No one pulled out a brown paper bag for entry!

To make a long story short, the three of us had one of the best times of our lives that night. I remember dancing out on the floor, and when I looked around, Ricky had this pretty Creole girl on his arm, and they were talking, smiling, laughing. When I turned around and looked over to where the chairs were, Ted, who never ever danced and was a gifted guitar player with no body rhythm and two left feet, was talking with another pretty Creole girl. These two Ninth Ward players "hooked up" with two pretty Creole girls. I was just hanging out, dancing and having a good time, and I did not even get a phone number that night, but Ted and Ricky walked out of there like two real Mack Daddies.

Ted and Ricky would eventually chat with those two girls over the phone for a couple of days. Before you knew it, the two backup gospel musicians were visiting the two Creole girls at their homes—times were a-changing.

While accompanying Ricky on his visit to this girl's house one evening when her parents were away, I witnessed her kissing him so aggressively I thought she was going to choke him. Then he stopped and sat up on the couch to catch his breath, but she pulled him back toward her even more aggressively and went at it again.

That is when I left the room and went outside to wait for Ricky. What I remember next is Ricky coming out of the house about one hour later, trying to catch his breath and looking as if he had been run over by a truck.

After that, without a question, there were not anymore gospel rehearsals or performances with the Big Brothers. Ted and Ricky were enjoying their new social circle.

New Orleans Police Harassment on Canal Street

On a sunny, pleasant afternoon in May of 1973, two New Orleans policemen decided to be belligerent. My sister graduated from Saint Mary's Academy in May of 1973. Ted and Ricky attended my sister's graduation with me that day at the New Orleans Municipal Auditorium, located in the Tremé neighborhood. After the graduation, my entire family,

Ted, Ricky, and I walked to my mom's car to put all my sister's trophies and awards—too many to count—in the car, but Ted, Ricky, and I did not get into the car to ride back home. We decided that we would walk a couple of blocks to Canal Street, hang out a while, and ride the RTA bus back home later that evening.

My mom said okay, so we said our goodbyes, and the three of us took off and walked a couple of blocks up to Canal Street. Remember, this is 1973; there were no suburban shopping malls yet, and Canal Street was the place for shopping, fast food, and hanging out.

The three of us were walking south on the east side of Canal Street on this beautiful late spring afternoon, enjoying ourselves, laughing, joking, and taking in the sights, just hanging out innocently, doing nothing wrong. There were no gang violence and major drug wars back then, at least not in the New Orleans that I was aware of; therefore, Canal Street was a very safe place to hang out. While walking, we decided to walk down to Werlein's for Music, a local music store. Let's just say this store was musicians' headquarters, where one could find anything from a small guitar pick to major sound systems.

Unexpectedly, a police car pulls up in the street and continues to move slowly toward us. We did not pay much attention because we knew we had done nothing wrong, so we just kept talking, walking, joking, and having a good time.

Then this police car turns on its patrol lights, pulls up directly on the side of the street where we are walking and parks. These two White cops jump out and tell us to stop walking and move back towards the building and stand against it. Again, this is May 1973. Canal Street was a thriving business area for people to shop and eat. "The hood," socially speaking, had not taken over Canal Street yet, not as it has today.

Well, here we go again. What else do three Black teenagers do when two White cops say, *"Stop walking, and move over towards the building"*?

We stopped and did what we were told.

Both cops came over, asked where we were coming from and where we were going. We told them politely, but they were still skeptical. As before, when I was detained after my school's fair, these policemen don't tell us why they are apprehending us. Two or three times, we asked why we were stopped. They did not answer us; they just proceeded to pat us down like criminals while hundreds of people on Canal Street looked on. They took our school IDs and went back to their cruiser.

As we stood there, hysterically wondering what the hell is going on, I remember looking over at Ricky's and Ted's faces and seeing fearful, terrifying expressions I had never seen on their faces before. The three of us just remained standing there, but we expressed to each other very quietly that this situation was bull.

Both cops eventually got out of the car after sitting in there for what seemed like twenty-four hours. They came over and explained to us that some guy who fit Ricky's description had robbed a store and gotten away. That was the biggest bullshit I'd ever heard. They gave us our IDs back.

One of the cops asked as he looked at me, *"So you go to Redemptorist Catholic High School and—*he turned to Ted and Ricky—*you two go to George Washington Carver High School?"*

"Yes," we replied.

The cop who'd asked the question just kept staring at me as if he could not understand how this one light complexion Creole kid could be friends with these two dark complexion Black kids. The two cops turned around, walked back to their car, and pulled off.

Strange, I guess the real reason they stopped us was because they could not understand how this Creole brother was hanging out with two "soul" brothers.

"Runaway Child, Running Wild"—The Temptations

Ricky and I started hanging out a lot more without the company of Ted because, again, Ted lived so far away. One Friday night at home, I was in bed at about 10:00 p.m., and I hear knocking at the back door. I get up to see who it is, and it is Ricky; he has run away from home. He got into an argument with his dad, the Reverend Williams; we called him Rev.

Now, Rev was about six feet eight inches tall and weighed about 260 pounds. If he wanted to trounce on a fifteen-year-old ninth grader, no problem—have your way, Rev.

To this day, I still do not know exactly what the argument was about, but Ricky's mother, Ms. Doris, phoned our house because she kind of speculated where Ricky ran off to. My mom told her it was okay for Ricky to sleep over that night until everything chilled out. Ricky slept over at our house that night and many other nights, and I used to sleep at his house now and then. When it was time for me to run away after a confrontation with my parents, I would go to Rickey's house too.

One night, I ran away after an argument, but I did not actually run. I drove away in my mom's car. I ran out of the house's front door after snatching the car keys sitting on the table, jumped in the car, and took off without a driving license. I did not bother to look at the gas needle to see how much gas was in the car as I was joyriding around. To my surprise, the car ran out of gas when I was about three miles from home. I had to walk all the way back home, scared as hell to face my mom.

When I arrived home, she fussed at me for running away and told me how irresponsible I was for taking the car without a driving license or permission from her. But she laughed about the fact that the car ran out of gas. Supposedly, I had learned my lesson, or did I?

War in City Park Stadium

Ricky and I went to an R&B concert; the band called War was playing at City Park Stadium with Billy Preston as the opening act. Later in life, I would meet Billy Preston for a day of adventure and long conversation that ended with "stay in school."

This was one of the first R&B concerts at City Park Stadium. I phoned two girls who were close friends and got Ricky and me dates for the night.

Yes, at fifteen years old, it was that easy for me back then to get a date.

I never forgot how people stared at Ricky and me while we walked around during the concert. Let me outline the situation. Back in the seventies, kids or teenagers did not wear sporty athletic jerseys of any kind—football, basketball, etc. That type of clothing was not in style yet, especially here in the South. If you wore any type of athletic jersey back then, you probably stole it from the school locker room.

Before the concert, Ricky and I went shopping, and there on the rack were these green-and-white New York Jets NFL-type football jerseys; those jerseys all were the same number, twelve—Broadway Joe Namath of the New York Jets, winner of the 1969 Super Bowl. Ricky and I thought these green-and-white jerseys were cool, so we decided to purchase one each and wear the matching jerseys to the concert with white pants.

Now that I look back at this, it was kind of despicable. We should not have done that, but we did. And now I know why everyone was looking at us "funny," excuse the pun. The two girls we double-dated with that night kept leaving us too. I could not figure out why back then, but now I know. Why would two Black guys dress identically alike in 1973 and go to an R&B concert? Ha ha ha ha!!!

The City Park concert was the first time Ricky and I saw War live. War was at the top of the R&B charts with several hits in 1973. Coincidentally, Ricky and I got a chance to physically meet the group again when my mom sneaked us into a small R&B banquet award show held at the Marriott Hotel on Canal Street.

Meeting the R&B Band War

My mom's best friend growing up was Jean Knight, or as we called her, Ms. Big Stuff, because in 1971 she had that big R&B hit "Mr. Big Stuff." We also called her Aint-Tee Jean.

Well, Ms. Jean was invited to participate in an R&B banquet that was being held in one of the ballrooms at the Marriott Hotel. Originally scheduled to perform for that event was Stevie Wonder, but Stevie had recently been involved in an automobile accident and could not perform, so the event organizers substituted the popular R&B group War.

Ms. Jean could not get us in the front door; however, my mom, having previously worked at the Marriott, knew some secret ways to get us in an adjacent room. My mom slipped us in through several passage ways throughout the hotel, and told us to stay put; once War started playing, she would come for us and get us closer to the stage.

So, Ricky and I are in the adjacent room anxiously waiting for the group War to go on stage to perform. We stayed there during the entire banquet event, while the awards were being given out, and through each speakers' and recipients' speeches.

At some point, Ricky and I needed to use the restroom, so off we went to find the bathroom. When we found it and opened the door, guess who was in the bathroom? WAR!!!! Yes, "Slipping Into Darkness," "Cisco Kid," and "Low Rider," preparing themselves to go onstage.

Do you really know what I mean when I say musicians are preparing to go onstage to perform? Just think about it.

There they were, the group War, one of the biggest R&B band groups in the summer of 1973. I remember those musicians as if it were yesterday. I got a chance to shake the hand of Lee Oskar, the harmonica player, who, because of that meeting, would eventually inspire me to start playing the harmonica.

So, there we were, two fifteen-year-old teenagers in the bathroom with War, and the smell of marijuana is everywhere. Ricky and I thought we had died and gone to heaven. We were talking and shaking their hands, and those group members started asking us how old we were and what our interests were once we graduated from high school. We told them we were musicians, and we loved listening and playing their music; we wanted to be recording musicians, like them. As the conversation continued, it got to be time for them to go onstage. They concluded the discussion regarding our future musical aspirations with the good old, customary celebrity response, *"Stay in school."*

Boring!!!!

I would eventually receive the same response from R&B recording artist Billy Preston, two years later, after spending an entire day driving him around New Orleans.

The Jackson 5—New Orleans Bands

My mom was socially connected to the music entertainment community through several close friends in addition to Ms. Jean. And because of that connection, my mom got a chance to meet many artists and managers of artists. One day, my mom received a phone call in which she was asked to reserve a gym that was equipped with a basketball floor and rims because the Jackson 5 needed a private place to play basketball upon their arrival in New Orleans later that week. They were to arrive the day before their concert, so their management team wanted to schedule activities for them so they would not have to just sit around in the hotel all evening.

My mom used her local connections and reserved the old Saint Mary's gym in the French Quarter. I called Ricky and explained the entire scenario to him, and he was excited.

Before I go on, I need to express my deepest opinion regarding the Jackson 5. I was no fan. Though I listened and danced to their music, I was not a big fan. I never even purchased a Jackson 5 album or 45 record. I cannot tell you why, but

I think it had to do with loving New Orleans's culture and music—R&B and funk.

During the Jackson 5's visit, the New Orleans live R&B and funk band era was at its peak. Why would someone be a big fan of five guys singing when you could play an instrument in a live band onstage in New Orleans, in the late sixties and seventies, during the time when live bands were worshipped? Just stop and think about what was happening in the R&B industry during the early seventies in regards to bands like War, the Isley Brothers, the Ohio Player, Kool and the Gang, and Earth, Wind & Fire, etc.

Here in New Orleans, we had the Meters, Chocolate Milk, Stop Inc., Trac One, Better Half, Louisiana Purchase, the Del-Rays, the Soul Sensation, and many, many others. The live band era took off in New Orleans in the seventies while R&B was booming, and funk was in the embryonic stages of explosiveness.

So, again, why would a young Black boy be a big fan of five guys singing onstage? That was for the girls. On top of that, I never ever remember any of the New Orleans live bands playing a Jackson 5 song. Honestly.

But there we were, Ricky and I, waiting for the Jackson 5 to show up at Saint Mary's old French Quarter gym to play basketball. We waited, waited, and waited. My mom was waiting too; she became impatient and decided to go place a phone call. Remember, there were no cell phones at the time, so my mom had to leave that location to go find a phone.

To make a long story short, while waiting for them over four or five hours, their plane was delayed, which meant they were several hours behind; therefore, we were asked to cancel the basketball event.

No problem. To this day, I have never regretted not meeting them, nor was I upset about their not showing up that night. But as I've gotten older, I've wondered what would or could have happened if I had had that chance to meet the Jackson 5. Ironically, twenty years later, my wife, my two kids, and I met the parents of the Jackson 5, Joe and Katherine Jackson, while eating lunch at Ralph and Kacoo's restaurant in a French Quarters, late 80's.

Ted, Ricky and I remained friends for years and experienced numerous incidents throughout high school and during my college years, as young men, which could be a book itself.

Chapter X

Uptown Ruler?

Not Me!!

Uptown New Orleans—A Strange Land

New Orleanians take pride in describing the neighborhoods in which they were raised, were educated, or are presently living. For example, some may say I am from Tremé, Bywater, Broadmoor, Gertown, Gentilly, the East, Carrollton, Holly Grove, Pontchartrain Park, Seventh Ward, etc. We could go on and on after naming about thirty or more neighborhoods. Then, there are the communities within some neighborhoods, such as Boscoville, the Goose, Back of Town, Pigeon Town, etc. And, believe it or not, New Orleanians take enormous pride in signifying their neighborhoods, just as people from Brooklyn, The Bronx or Queens, New York, will let you know it frequently during a conversation.

The readers of this book already know I lived in several neighborhoods from birth through my high school years, so it is hard for me to identify with just one area. But the only one that has remained in my heart all these years is the Ninth Ward because we lived in the Lower Ninth Ward, the Upper Ninth Ward, and eventually Eastern New Orleans, which is the Ninth Ward. Even today, when someone as ask which area of the city I am from, my response is the Ninth Ward, with Seventh Ward experiences.

However, I have identified with the Ninth Ward traditional slogan "I am from the Nine and don't mind dying."

We moved uptown and lived there for one year on Jena Street. I can justifiably say I am not and never was an Uptown Ruler. That title was often cried out by Cyril Neville of the local R&B bands The Meters and the Neville Brothers; you can hear that lyrics in the Meters' song "Hey Pocky A-Way."

Uptown in New Orleans is geographically the area west of Canal Street, and though Uptown New Orleans represents financial success and has numerous wealthy neighborhoods along Saint Charles Avenue and in the Garden District, an Uptown Ruler was not from those wealthy areas of Uptown. Rather, it is a description of a person from the less affluent communities of Uptown, like Cabbage Alley and or Central City. That description had nothing to do with violence, gangs, or thugs, as some people today have tried to associate it with. It was just Cyril Neville's way of taking pride in the fact that he was from Uptown, and he is the definitive, all proclaimed "Uptown Ruler."

Our Jena Street house, our "home away from home."

In the late summer of '73, we moved from Law Street in the Ninth Ward, from our nice, small brick home to a wooden shotgun double on Jena Street, at the corner of South Lopez Street. It was in the Broadmoor neighborhood, in the middle of Uptown, right off Fontainebleau Drive, three blocks from Nashville Avenue.

At the time, my sister was in college at LSU as a freshman. Lucky her, she never had to live Uptown. But when she came home that Thanksgiving and Christmas break, 1973, it was different from coming home to Law Street, where for the last six years of her and my life we had lived. She did not like Uptown, and neither did I, for, indeed, it was a strange land.

For the life of me, I do not know what got into the mind of my mom to move us from downtown into this strange land. Though, while living on Law Street, there were some older guys I socialized with who had a big influence on my social behavior.

Broadmoor was ninety-nine percent middle-class White. We all know New Orleanians take pride in their neighborhoods, high schools, and local communities, and those places help us to identify who and what we are or what our values and social classifications represent. My idea of home was either the Seventh or Ninth Ward, and there was no area in Uptown where I had a passion to live.

However, as a fifteen-year-old, what do you do when your parents move?

There is only one thing to do, and that is to follow. This was one of those unfortunate things I had to do—live in Uptown New Orleans. There was nothing about Uptown that I liked.

Alcee Fortier High School

Our new home location was in the Alcee Fortier High School District, and the school year was about to start. We had no idea what to expect and had no relevant academic or social information about the school because we were new to Uptown. We had heard from associates that Fortier was an acceptable school to attend, and I was determined not to go back to Redemptorist. I didn't want to enroll in Saint Augustine High School either because I could not bear the thought of being in school all day without girls. Therefore, I convinced my mom to enroll me at Fortier. So it was off to school on the first day, and what a first day it would be.

On that first day of school at Fortier, it was raining extremely hard; therefore, instead of riding the bus or walking, my mom decided to drive me to school. We drove up Nashville Avenue to South Claiborne Avenue, and at the Regional Transit bus stop, there were tens of students waiting in the rain to catch the bus. Some of them had umbrellas, and five or six students were trying to stand under one umbrella.

My mother, being the Good Samaritan or nice person that she always was, and still is, decided to pull over to the bus stop. It is on my side of the car, so I have no idea what she is about to do. I am thinking she is going to let me out here to catch the bus with the rest of the kids in the rain because I had an umbrella. But instead, she asked me roll down the car window; then she leans over me, sticks her head out the window, and screams, *"Does anyone want a ride to school?"*

See, back in the seventies, it was the norm for one Black person to offer another Black person a ride without knowing that person. This is New Orleans; there is no kidnapping or major crimes happening. It was a good place to live, other than some racial tensions. And as Black people, we were all clients of the bus system for school, work, church, or socializing. We were just Black people trying to help each other endure.

These two guys accepted her invitation for the ride, so I opened the back door and they jumped in the car. Now we have two real Uptown Rulers sitting in our back seat, and these two guys are tough-looking, but cool dudes as I would later find out after getting to know them.

Alcee Fortier High School, Ferret Street, New Orleans, Louisiana.

During the conversation while driving to school, I found out these two guys, Tyrus and Dillion, are seniors. Then, as the school year progressed, I discovered they were social leaders in school. In other words, no one ever troubled with these two guys. They were not bad dudes, from what I knew, but I did not know them personally. They did not cause trouble in school, but they were highly respected. I do not know how their lives were within their neighborhoods or communities, so maybe there was some things about them that I did not know, but in school, they were cool cats.

Good Looking Out for Me, Mom

As I was sitting in the front seat of the car, embarrassed because my mom was driving me to school and they were catching the bus, and because I was dressed neater than these two guys on the first day of school, I did not realize that my future destiny had already traversed time. That day, my mom's pre-destined goodness to help others by offering a ride ended up saving me from many fights, beatdowns, and possibly death. Were these two guys my two angels, Mercy and Grace?

It is amazing how the universe works. But when you are young, you do not know how one decision or event, meeting someone or making friends, can one day in the future save your butt. Life is an experience teacher.

Let me make an analogy of this situation. Meeting and making friends with these two guys was similar to my getting arrested, walking into prison, and finding out these two prison-gang rulers are now my best friends, so now in prison, I'm protected, and no one can mess with me. It was like that for me. With these two guys in my corner, I made it through that tough school year. They called me by the same nickname my step-grandfather gave me, but they left off the word "dirty" and only referred to me as Red. Wow, as if I had not been called that before. Now, everyone in school was referring to me as Red.

Mercy and Grace or Tyrus and Dillion—Almost Stabbed

While attending Fortier, I was the normal high school student making friends, more female than male. There were not many light-complexion or Creole students at Fortier, just a handful because most of the Creole and light-complexion Black culture was downtown. Facts are facts, end of conversation.

I started chatting with this one girl who was on the track team. She was a cute, dark-complected girl, and she told me that she and her old boyfriend, who was literally a thug, had split up. I came to find out later that, in her mind, they had split up, but in his mind, based on his actions, he mentally had not split up with her.

One school day while I was in the bathroom, this same thug guy is on one side of the bathroom, smoking a cigarette, and I am on the other side, using the facilities. He shouts out to the other boys in the restroom, *"Hey, y'all, see RED. He took ma gurl fend fum me."*

I turned to him and asked, *"Who yaw girlfriend is?"*

To my surprise, he said the name of the same girl that I had been talking to. I was stunned that she was still going out with this guy. Damn, she had poor taste. He and I then exchanged some he-said, she-said stuff.

I finally said, *"No, bra, I did not steal ha from yaw. She say y'all broke up. I did not steal ha from yaw."*

Oh my God, what did I just say? I hope the angels are on their way from heaven to rescue me because I know something bad is about to happen.

I am just standing there, eye-to-eye contact, and this guy is getting very angry. We don't say a word to each other for about ten or fifteen seconds; he is not responding, and I am waiting for him to respond. I continue to stare him down, and then I realize this guy not only has this dating issue, but he is high on some kind of drug or he's drunk.

He begins to move towards me, and as he gets closer, he reaches down into his pants pocket and pulls out something that looks like a knife. But it is not a knife; it's worse. It's a very pointy industrial ice pick. I just stand there. Time has literally stopped, and there is not a sound in that bathroom; everyone in the bathroom is looking on, and no one is making a sound. I remained standing there, frozen, looking at him and not knowing what to do. He continues to approach me with the ice pick in his hand, waving it in front of my face-, while verbally describing how he is going to stab and cut me up it I don't stay away from his girlfriend.

Just then, my "two angels" literally arrived. The two guys whom my mom picked up on the first day of school, Tyrus and Dillion, "coincidentally" walked into the bathroom and saw what was going on; they immediately jumped into the middle of the action and asked what the hell was going on. They started pushing the other guy back against the wall, and then they took the ice pick out of his hand.

Once Tyrus and Dillion intervened on my behalf, I ran out the bathroom as if I were a cat escaping hell. I knew I would see those two somewhere later, so I was sure they did not mind my running out of there like a little wimp.

Question? My two angels, Mercy and Grace, were they disguised as the two guys, Tyrus and Dillion? Because Tyrus and Dillion never talked about or mentioned that situation after that, NEVER. And I do not remember seeing Tyrus and Dillion in school earlier that day.

That thug guy who pulled the ice pick on me never talked to or bothered me again.

Mercy And Grace—Accepting Ride Home

My Uptown friends and Fortier High School functions were really starting to bore me, and I needed to go back downtown to hang out with my old friends.

I rode the city bus one Friday night from our Uptown home on Jena Street to go to a Saint Aug football game at City Park Stadium. Even when I lived downtown, catching the bus every Friday evening during football season to go a Saint Aug football game on Friday nights was a religious ritual.

On this Friday night after the game, I convened with some downtown friends, and we ended up at this girl's home in Gentilly for a house party, and then she and her friends told us about another house party in the East. While at this party in the East, I found a ride over to another house party in Press Park, the Upper Ninth Ward.

My poor mom, I am sure she had no idea where I was, and I never called home to check in with her or asked her to come and pick me up. She just trusted me to make the right decisions.

I was having a good time on this Friday night, to the point that I did not realize how fast the time passed. The next thing I knew, it was 2:00 a.m., and the friends I went to that party with had already left without telling me. I had to figure out how to get home. I was only three or four blocks away from my friend Rickey's home, but, again, it was two in the morning, and I did not want to awaken him and his family. Reverend Williams (Rev), Ricky's dad, would have kicked my butt that night had I woken them up at 2:00 a.m.

So, brave me, I walked about a mile to catch the bus at Louisa Street and Chef Menteur, US-Hwy 90. It was now 2:30 a.m. I am standing there waiting on a bus. I am about seven miles from home at about 2:30 a.m., and there is no bus in sight. I should have just gone to Ricky's house, let Rev hassle me for waking them up, and called my mom to let her know I was sleeping there. But I did not do that.

Luckily, this is an early fall night in September, and it is warm. As I am standing there waiting for the bus, about an hour passes, and the time is now 3:30 a.m., and there is not a car on the street. Then, literally out of nowhere, a car is heading west on Chef Menteur, US Highway 90, and it stops at the red light in front of me while I am standing at the bus stop. The car sits there at the traffic light for about one minute, and right as the traffic light turns green, one of the three Black guys in the car shouts, *"Hey, bra, you need a ride? Yaw know, it's three in da mornen, and ain't no buses comin'. Do yaw need a ride?"*

So, brave me, I respond, *"Yeah, bra, I need a ride."*

At that point, all I knew was that I needed to get home. I had accepted rides from strangers before; those experiences were not all bad. Therefore, I knew how to protect myself, but not against three guys. I took my chances anyway.

I got into the car, scared and skeptical, and sat in the back on the right side, close to the door, my hand on the handle just in case I need to open it and jump out. The driver started talking about how late it was and that only one bus was running on the Chef Menteur—the US Highway 90/Broad Street line—during that time of morning, and that route was about a thirty-mile round trip for that bus. I sat there quietly, and they asked where I was going. So I told them, and they offered to take me all the way home.

I was really scared, and I held the handle of the door as if it were my life source. The driver kept talking and talking, and the other two guys started talking too. They said they recognized me from one of the parties we were at that night, but, honestly, I did not remember seeing those guys at any of the parties I attended earlier that night. Thank God they recognized me and offered me a ride.

I was starting to feel less worrisome after the conversation. So I offered to buy them some gas. The driver was elated; he pulled into the station. I put three dollars of gas in the car; that was almost half a tank back then at fifty-five cents a gallon. We pulled out of the station, and they drove me all the way to my front door, like good Samaritans.

Amazing. Can you imagine taking a ride with three guys you do not know anything about at 3:30 a.m. in the morning today?

Those three guys were probably my angels once again. My angels, Mercy and Grace, had a friend with a car, and they said, *"Let's go take Herman home."*

Derrick: St. Augustine Band Member, My Friday Night Hero

While still attending Fortier, in my uptown neighborhood there were these three guys I used to hang out with that lived over on Calhoun St. that attended St. Aug High School.

In the 70's, I loved and still love the Black Exploitation movies. I have seen almost all of them; the first of many, Sweet, Sweet Back Bad Ass, follow up by Shaft, Black Cesar, Super Fly, The Mack, Coffey, Foxy Brown, Three the Hard Way, Truck Turner, etc. I was very fond of these movies and looked upon the actors as heros. In my silly way of imagining myself, I wanted to be like them, or experienced what they experienced. In a sense, they, the actors were my heroes, and to see black people on a big movie screen in, '72, '73, '74, in one of the nice move theaters like the Orpheum, Joy or Sanger was enough to make a young person believe he or she could achieve more in life. But those fictionist characters never really came close to my true hero. A St. Augustine High School band member named Derrick.

Derrick was the older brother of one kid I used to hang out with uptown. Derrick played trumpet in the band, and he was a senior, so, this was his year to graduate, spring '74. Derrick owned and drove a Maroon Chevrolet/Camaro, 1968. This guy thought he was a lover or playa, meaning, he thought he could get any girl he wanted. But maybe that was true, because back then, if you were a black guy with any kind of a car in the '70's, one could classify themself as a lover or playa, and again, but only if you had a car. And if you were lucky to have a car, then you probably would not have a problem getting a date. My Aunt Melva dated a very unattractive guy in her senior year, 1969. I remember vividly her response to one of her friends when asked, why are you dating that guy? Her response, *"he got a car gurl."*

On the other hand, if you had to catch the bus like myself, before and after a house party, school dances or high school football games, then it would be hard to date or take a girl on a date while riding the bus.

On one of my most unforgettable Friday nights, fall 1973, I was a sophomore, and after a St. Aug football game, my hero Derrick would get a very sweet creole surprise.

It was a Friday night and St. Aug. would have dances after the football games in the school's gym. I was standing out in front of the gym just hanging out with one of Derricks's brothers and several other friends from uptown that needed a ride home after the dance ended around 11pm. We were having a good time after the dance contemplating catching the bus home because we did not know of anyone that would give all of us a ride home in a car. We were either going to catch the bus home or hitch a ride, because uptown to Jena St. was just too far of a walk, so we were trying to see if we could luck up and catch a ride with someone.

As we are standing there, Derrick pulls up in his 1968 Camaro in front of the gym, parks his car, then he gets out of the car, walks over and hang out a while with us, then he inter-acts around with other friends and several group of friends. Derrick was like the ring leader in his social circle of "pretty boys" and he seemed to know everybody on this night. I just stood there and watched how he maneuvered his way back and forth between different groups of students...he knew everyone and he was the coolest. I said to my 15-year old self, I want to be like that when I am senior. After Derrick stopped with his social exchanges, he realized that nothing was happening for him because most of the girls had already gone home and those that were there were with their boy-friends, so he offered us a ride home, nice guy, I like this dude. So, six of us jump into the car, three in the back seat, three in the front: I am sitting in the window passenger seat. We were being cramped up together like sardines in a con-tainer but that didn't matter, we were getting a ride home, no bus ride tonight - *Mercy and Grace, you can take the night off.*

Right when we are driving off in the car, appearing out of nowhere, there she is...... "Annette Dupree." Now, Annette Dupree, is not just any high school girl, "SHE IS THE GIRL" that every guy would love to take out on a date. Annette is a very beautiful fair complexion CREOLE girl with green pretty eyes, long light brown hair, and she is shaped like a coke bottle with above average breast for a girl 15 or 16 years old. Lets just say when someone decided to describe women with curves, they were envisioning Annette Dupree. Annette attracts all of the attention when in her company. She has that magic, the curves, the eyes, and beauty.

Derrick looks to the right of his car while pulling off and out of the window he notices Annette talking to some other students. I'm looking at her too, I am a 15-year-old boy, it's impossible not to see her, she's beautiful...and mature. Yes, she has her way with the boys. I am thinking to myself, while sitting there in the car, *"I sure wish I had a car tonight for just me and Annette."* As I am sitting there in my on imaginary world thinking about Annette and I and how we could make our on Black Exploitation movie, Derrick unexpectedly pulls over to the side of the street where Anette is, stops the car, bends over from the driver side of the car, leans over the guy in the middle seat and leans over me against the door and shouts at Annette to get her attention. She turns around, smiling and giggling and starts approaching the car and as she gets to the car, she bends over to lean on the window to see into the car *(and everything is visible, the word cleavage was created because if her.)* She starts flirting back with Derrick and me. Now remember, I am sitting in the front (scrub seat) and she is bending over with her two hands on the car talking back and forth with Derrick. She has on a lowcut blouse on and I hardly looked up while she and Derrick was having this conversation. WHAT CONVERSA-TION? She and I made thrilling flirtation eye contact a couple of times, and I honestly believe she was purposely giving me the "free look pass." I am sure the guys in the back seat were looking at the dividing line on her chest too. I guess we guys in the car "were not" paying attention or listening to the conversation between Derrick and Annette because all of us, our attention was on her cleavage. She and Derrick shared in conversation for about one minute, and for one minute,

I can't tell you what her and Derrick discussed because I was having a fantasy Black Exploitation movie love scene in my mind evolving her and me. The title of that imaginary movie, "Cleavage Conqueror."

Then she pops the question of the night that everyone wanted hear. *"Derrick, can you give me a ride home, I need a ride home, please?"* That was the only thing I heard her say. At that point I envisioned Annette sitting on my lap because there was no other place in the car for her to sit. Please, please, Derrick, say yes.

You should have seen the expression on Derrick's face after that question. We could easily make room for Annette to get in this car, no problem, as a matter of fact; she could sit on my lap. I am excessively thinking, PLEASE… say yes. I was going to be a nice young man and make room for Annette and let her sit in the seat with me, or on my lap in this front seat, and I think she wanted to sit on my lap, because she saw the car was crowded, any that would be the only place for her to sit.

Derrick responded…yes…,(thank you JESUS) … and I got all excited, because I had the seat for her to sit in.

I DID NOT ANTICIPATE WHAT WAS ABOUT TO HAPPEN NEXT, AFTER HE SAID YES TO ANNETTE.

Derrick jumps out of the driver seat side of the car and started screaming at the top of his lungs while waving his arm like a policeman on street patrol giving arm signal directions:

OUT!!!! OUT!!!! OUT!!!!!
ALL YA'LL "LIL" MOTHERS GET OUT OF THE CAR.
GET THE HELL OUT OF MY CAR………RIGHT NOW!!!!
YA'LL GO CATCH THE BUS HOME..!!

We could not believe we had to get out of the car. WHY...? I was all prepared for Annette to sit on my lap and I think she was ready to sit on my lap too, based on the eye contact we made. I did not anticipate Derrick's reaction to her question of needing a ride home. Unfortunately for me and the other guys, we all got out and Annette got into the car while making eye contact with me once again, as in saying, "I did not think Derrick was going to kick you out of the car." But I am sure a ride home for her was more important than me staying in the car. They drove off into the night and we all stood there looking at each other wondering what the hell just happen.

I honestly believe Annette did not think Derrick was going to kick us or me out of the car when she asked for a ride home. I think she was ready to sit next to me or on my lap. None of us perceived his future actions.

Damn!!!!!! Now we had to catch the bus home.... AGAIN.

We still could not believe he kicked us out of the car as we walked to the bus stop. We shared some wonderfully fantasy stories involving Annette, had we been in Derrick's shoes that night. TRULY and HONESTLY...I would have done the same thing if I had been in his shoes.

He did the right thing, in the right situation, on the right night, at the right time, and any boy that is a senior in high school would have done the same thing. Especially having a chance to give Annette Dupree a ride home after the dance. Derrick, my Friday night hero.

And in concluding, Annette Dupree and I would "hook up"- date, later as seniors while attending the same high school.

I Saved a True Purple Knight

Uptown on Jena Street and living in Broadmoor was becoming a real drag, and as the school year of 1973-74 was coming to an end at Fortier, it was not coming fast enough. It is springtime and high school basketball season is in full swing. Saint Aug's basketball team visited Fortier gym to play against them. That night something happened to me that drove a stick straight into my heart; it still has a lingering influence on my life today.

The JV game was being played, and I knew several of the kids who were on Saint Aug's team. The kid I had a fight with in fourth grade at Epiphany, the Fight of the Decade, was a member of Saint Aug's JV basketball team too. We, the Fortier students, those Uptown Rulers, were up in the bleaches, cheering our team on while the junior varsity game was being played. Saint Aug won the JV game, and during intermission between the junior varsity and varsity games, we students went outside to hang out in front of the gym before the varsity game started.

The Fortier gym was very old, and the water fountains were on the outside of the building. The Saint Aug JV team did not have a watercooler on their bench for their players, so one of the Saint Aug JV players decided to come outside to get a drink of water at the conclusion of the JV game while we Fortier students were outside. What happened next shocked the hell out of me.

As this intelligent Black, African American student, a member of the Saint Aug JV team, went to get a drink of water from one of the outside fountains, the Fortier students, some of my friends who were outside with me, started violently tantalizing, teasing, and provoking this Saint Aug player. Verbally harassing this kid, his teammates, his parents, his

Creole heritage, and verbally demeaning and belittling the entire Saint Aug school and student body. They called this kid every vulgar title you can think of, and they referred to his mother with such vulgarity. Why? She was not even there.

I could not comprehend nor believe what I was hearing and seeing. I did not know why we needed to hate on a Saint Aug student, the school, or the parents of the students. It was unbelievable for me. I stood there, and as I heard all of this vulgarity, I wanted to tell all of the Fortier students to "shut the F*** up," but I couldn't, for fear of retaliation towards me. Remember, I was the exception to the rule at Fortier; there were only a couple of light complexion Creole people in the school.

Though I did not know this Saint Aug basketball player personally, the one at whom all the vulgarity was being directed, I had seen him around at different parties and functions, so he was a social friend. Therefore, I intrinsically sided with him, and I knew at that moment I needed to figure out how to protect him. I felt his pain, literally.

I wanted to say to all the Fortier Uptown Rulers, *"Hey, it's 1974. Aren't we in this world together as Black people, struggling, trying to make things better for all Black people?"*

Yes, I used to go to elementary school with some of the Saint Aug students. And yes, they were spoiled brats back then when they were young. But they are Black, and we are Black, so why am I about to witness Black-on-Black crime for no reason whatsoever? It can't be just about light complected skin, right?

Social Class—Light-Complexion Black versus Dark-Complexion Black—For Real? In 1974?

I was not going to allow the Fortier students to physically beat down this kid; I felt his pain. So, as the Fortier students stood there harassing this kid, and as he was backing up against the wall, I slowly started to push my way to the front of the crowd because I needed to side with my Fortier schoolmates, and I needed to save this kid's butt. I needed to get up in front of this confrontation, just in case something physical would start to happen; then I could stop it.

The Saint Aug JV player looked towards the crowd around him with fear on his face; then he and I made eye contact, and he recognized my face. I could see him looking towards me, his eyes saying, *"Bra, help me out here."* I continued to make small steps towards him, and finally I was in the front, standing between him and the crowd. Without saying a word, I just stood there as a barricade between him and this violent crowd, protecting him silently. He looked at me again, and then he looked back up at the vulgar crowd as they continued to verbally harass him.

Slowly, he started moving towards the door to go back into the gym. The crowd moved too, and I kept my body between him and the crowd close to him. He was looking down as he walked to the door, but he finally made it back into the gym.

I have to give this brother credit for his bravery because when he turned around from that drinking fountain and saw those guys approaching him, he did not back down or run back into the gym. He stood there and started balling his hands into fists, ready to fight. He was not going to start anything, but he was determined and ready to stand his ground and defend himself.

He was a…true…Purple Knight!!!!!! I was his Mercy and Grace, his angel on this night, protecting him from this display of polluted, illiterate, ignorance.

At that moment, I completely grasped that there were major racial-class differences in the Black community that I had never fully comprehended as a young kid, until this incident. For me, a young sixteen-year-old, this situation was very bizarre and perplexing because it was exactly one year ago that I had a speech contest stolen from me at an all-White school, and I had a White kid, the senior running back football player at Redemptorist Catholic High School, almost knock every bone out of my body because of my Afro.

All that happened just one year ago, in the spring of 1973. And now, a year later, in the spring of 1974, I am standing here, watching young Black men team up and rudely pester another young Black man just because of the differences in skin pigmentation. For Real….?

WHAT THE HELL IS GOING ON?!!!!!

I was so discouraged and mortified at this situation that I did not go back into the gym to watch the varsity game. I turned around and went home. I was hurt that night because my own Black schoolmates had tried to destroy another Black man.

I could not believe what just happened, and the only thing I was looking forward to was leaving Fortier. I needed and wanted to get out of that school quickly.

After that event, when I attended school for the remainder of that year, I stopped hanging out with everyone. Instead, I retreated to a back hallway, back in the corner of the building, away from all the other students until the morning bell rang for homeroom. I did not want to mingle or be friendly with anyone at Fortier High School after that incident. I and this other guy who didn't like Fortier either would just hang out there until the morning bell rang, then go to class, go to lunch, hang out in the same back corner at lunchtime, and then head straight home after school. I completely stopped socializing at Fortier. I could not wait for the school year to come to an end, and that end did not come soon enough.

All my life, from both White and Black teachers, I was constantly encouraged to receive a quality education and to become a productive, accountable citizen. And when I did that, still, there was discrimination? Unbelievable.

I dare someone say I had a choice in picking my skin tone. That is absurd. If I did, then every other person born would have the same choice too, right? While in our mothers' wombs, we all can choose to be White, Black, Indian, Asian, etc. That's how it would be if that absurdity were a reality.

Stop the bigotry, racial discrimination, and prejudices on this planet, PERIOD!!! We are all created in the image of God. Therefore, let us seek what that image is and work towards perfecting that image.

Gypsy Man

Later that spring, right before school ended, which seemed to drag on and on, the music department/band, had a spring performance for the entire student body in the gym. I was not a member of the school's marching band, but during my fourth period music class, we studied music composition, coordination, pitch, etcetera. As a result, I was able to practice on my trumpet during the class and sharpen my music skills every day. That spring, the R & B group WAR, (my favorite band), whom I had already met personally, had another very big R & B hit song. The song was titled *"GYPSY MAN"* and it played on local radio often and it was a big hit. Because I was a big War fan, I decided to purchase a harmonica, being inspired by Lee Oskar, the harmonica player for the group War, and see if I could play the harmonica solo part in the song "Gypsy Man," and other group songs that had harmonica solos, like The Doobie Brothers, "Long Train Runnin," for example. To my surprise, I mastered the harmonica solo piece easily in "Gypsy Man."

One day while in music class, a couple days before the school band performed in the gym. The music Director/Teacher, Mr. Gonzales on an earlier occasion, had asked our class to bring one of our favorite LPs to music class because he wanted to see what our personal music interest were. Well, I didn't bring War, I brought another album, a group called "MANDRILL" – they had two songs that were hot in 1974 too. One titled "FENCE WALK" and the other was "HANG LOOSE." Another student brought War, the LP that featured "Gypsy Man." During class the teacher asked us to play one or two of our favorite songs from our own LP. Everyone played theirs and I played mine. The music teacher was fascinated with my choice because he said he had never heard of Mandrill or those songs. After listening to just about everyone's music the only person left was the student that brought the War LP, so the teacher played the LP. I regularly carried my harmonica with me in a little gray leather pouch that hung from my blue jeans belt loop, like a hippy, trying to look like Lee Oskar, because I was a big War fan. Remember those blue jeans I mentioned that I purchased from Krauss for $1 back in chapter two? I wore those just about every day during my sophomore year of high school until the threads fell apart.

Now the song "Gypsy Man" is being played on the "record player," and as we are all listening, I decided to pull out my harmonica to play the harmonica solo part when the song gets to that point. No one knows what I am about to do, so the song gets to the solo part, then I start performing simultaneously along with the song. The music teacher and everyone in the class looked over to me with amazement as I played along, note-to-note, timing perfectly. After the song and I finished, Mr. Gonzales wanted to know how and when did I got interested in playing the harmonica. I told him, earlier that year when I heard "Gypsy Man" on the radio. I told him I went out and purchased a harmonica just to see if I could play those harmonica parts. Mr. Gonzales was so impressed with my playing of the solo part in the song that after class he pulled me to the side to talk and suggested that I perform that solo part with the band during the upcoming spring performance in the gym that coming Friday. The Fortier's school marching band had already been playing "Gypsy Man" as one of their musical selections. I wasn't sure about performing because I had not practiced with the band. He told me, you don't need to practice with us, just play what you already know. He wanted me to play the solo part in the song at the end of the song as the band backed me up.

This is how it was going to be set up. There was going to be a microphone in front of the band on a mic stand and I was to stand and wait in the back until the very end of the song when the harmonica solo came up. No one in the audience was going to know about my solo harmonica performance, it was going to be a surprise to the staff and student body. No one knew I was going to do this except one guy that played bass drum in the band. He was in our fourth period music class, so he overheard Mr. Gonzales asking me to perform the solo. I wished the music teacher would have let me practice with the band so that I could get my timing and "ear tone" down packed, but that never happened, because again Mr. Gonzales wanted this performance to be a surprise.

The day of the performance came. The gym was packed with the student body, staff, and teachers. I was standing in the back of the band the entire time during several songs and just waiting for the band to play "Gypsy Man." I figured Mr. Gonzales would wait to perform that song last and that is just what happened. After about eight or nine songs, my nerves are going crazy, and now the band finally played the song. The microphone is up front, the music teacher looks at me, standing in the back, I looked at him, and it's on now. I looked over to the bass drum player and he started motioning me to go up to the microphone and just stand there until the solo part comes. All I was thinking about was I did not get a chance to rehearse with the band, which I really needed and wanted to do, just for tone/pitch quality purposes. I could have performed that solo perfectly, just like I presented the poem "Annabelle Lee' in ninth grade "perfectly" and that was because I practiced, practiced, rehearsed.

But there I stood, as the band played the song, frozen in time and space like a statue. I just did not have an ear for it and the band sounded as if they were in a different key. I could not get my body to move towards the front of the band and walk up to the microphone. The harmonica solo part of the song came, I am still standing like a frozen statue. As I looked around, I knew word had spread to several other members in the band that I was supposed to walk up now and perform the harmonica solo part, because they started looking at me as in saying, *"why aren't you walking up to the microphone?"* I am FROZEN, LIKE A BLOCK OF ICE, COULDN'T MOVE. I just didn't feel the presence/spirit of the music like I felt when I would hear it played on the record player at home, or on the radio. Was I scared, yes. I was scared I was going to make a mistake for not practicing with the band. To me, hearing this song while the band played it, in this wide-open gym, the sound just wasn't the same, and I didn't really want to embarrass myself by going up to that microphone and being OUT OF KEY and or OUT OF RHYTHM because that would have been worst. Being out of key or off rhythm was more important to me than my reputation of being a coward or having a lack of confidence, and yes, I did lack confidence because of no rehearsal. If I had practiced/rehearse one time with the band or a couple of practices before this performance, I would have played the harmonica solo. Well, I never went up to the microphone and the band continued to play the song to the end. To my surprise, no one in the band criticized me after I explained to them why I did not approach the microphone to play the solo, because they were musicians and they understood, PRACTICE makes perfect.

It has puzzled me for many years as to why I could not push myself to perform that harmonica solo, and every time I hear that song, it sends me back to a "photo memory," standing behind the band, frozen. Now that I look back, here is what I believe happened that did not allow me to go up to that mic and perform the Gypsy Man harmonica solo.

Traditionally, people of Gypsy culture are often looked upon as outsiders. I was an outsider in the strange land of Uptown New Orleans. I was not an "Uptown Ruler." For me to go up to that mic and perform the Gypsy Man's harmonica solo would have solidified my association with Uptown culture/community which I was not a part of. If I had performed that solo, I would have been an icon in the school and probably titled the nickname, "Gypsy Man from Uptown." New Orleanians have a way of titling people with nicknames. After all that I had experienced at Fortier good and bad, I needed to remain as an outsider and not leave anything behind that people would remember me by or that would validate me as being from Uptown. 50 years later, if I had played that solo, I could hear someone saying, *"there was this dude I went to school with at Fortier, Gypsy Man, from uptown......he played the War - Gypsy Man harmonica solo during one of Fortier's high school band spring performances."*

Nothing wrong with Uptown or people from Uptown, there are a lot of good people and places in Uptown. All communities/neighborhoods throughout New Orleans have unique challenges regarding culture, community, religion, education, and crime. But this one person, "me" was not from Uptown. I assure you, before the 80's, for most Black individuals, you could not get a person who was born, raised, and educated in Uptown to say they were from Downtown and or vice/versa. We did not move or relocate, Downtowners/ Uptowners, to either community, facts are facts. Even after growing up, and becoming professional educated people, we preferred to stay and live in the community where we had family, friends, and attended church before the 80's. Professional careered individuals and/or other hardworking labor force adults would reside in a house or apartment in the community in which they grew up close to their relatives. We did not move "across town" to another completely different world. It was just part of that New Orleans way of life, where we took pride in our neighborhood upbringing. Today, it is different, and multiple social and economic dynamics have contributed to the change in neighborhoods/communities: crime, housing, and the Government Housing Assistance Section 8 program, changed New Orleans and without doubt, Eastern New Orleans.

We eventually moved back to the Ninth Ward in Eastern New Orleans, or as the locals say it, New Orleans East, in the spring of 1974. That spring I turned sixteen years old and got my driver's license. I would eventually attend a new high school in the fall of 1974, Eleanor McMain Magnet High School, for my junior and senior years. My life would undeniably move in a different direction that I will cover in *"Creole Boy Two—Uncensored."*

Chapter XI

My Sister

Big Dee

There are TOO MANY stories from my entire life that I can share about my sister and me. So, in this chapter, I will try to highlight those special incidents that had major influences or that were of emotional significance in our lives.

My sister passed away from cancer on October 4, 2019, at the age of sixty-four. Therefore, I dedicate this entire chapter to my sister because, without her, I probably would not have made it through some challenging situations, especially when we lived in the Desire Housing Project.

We would argue constantly and sometimes over the simplest thing. This is normal behavior for brothers and sisters at home, but out in the streets, away from home, if you messed with my sister, I would try to kick your butt. If someone tried to make trouble for me, my sister would kick their butt. That's just the way it was—we were FAMILY!

My sister was not fat; she was just a big-boned girl. As I mentioned earlier, the kids in our community of the Ninth Ward called her Big Dee.

My sister was like my bodyguard as we grew up. She always referred to me as her baby brother, and I always referred to her as my big sister. As we became older adults, I changed that around and started referring to her as my baby sister because she was my only sister; I also said that I was her big brother because I was her only brother. Just a play on words, but we had fun with it.

I have already shared some of our experiences, but I want to use this chapter to express my deepest feelings and thoughts I have for my sister. She was always the bright, intelligent one because she was the oldest. But smartness and playfulness are two different things. I have already shared a story in chapter one about how she almost drowned in Miami. What every entered her clever head that day, I have no idea.

Two Lost Negro Kids

One day, I trusted my smart sister to make a right decision, but she did not. I started crying out of fear because we were lost and nearly did not make it home.

My sister was in the fifth grade, and I was in second. We had to catch the city bus home from school one day. Our home was below or east of the industrial canal in the Lower Ninth Ward, on Alabo Street. I was just this naïve second grader who had no idea what was going on; I just trusted and knew my sister would make the right decisions.

We boarded the Louisa Street bus, then rode the distance to our destination, where we would transfer to the Galvez Street bus. There were two Galvez Street bus routes that had two different final destinations; one had a longer route and went farther into the Lower Ninth Ward neighborhoods, and the other one stopped at France Street and did not go over the industrial canal bridge farther into the Lower Ninth Ward.

We somehow ended up on the short-routed bus, and when that bus arrived at the route's end, France Street, everyone exited, and we were instructed to get off too. I remember how frightened my sister was. I remember the two of us just standing on the side of the street like refugees.

The bus driver, a genuinely nice White gentleman, noticed and perceived my sister had selected the wrong bus route. He came over and spoke to my sister and me, asking what our destination was. She explained to him our situation, and that very kind bus driver stopped the next bus, which happened to be the correct Galvez Street bus that had the longer Lower Ninth Ward destination route.

The bus driver who was helping us stepped up into that bus, and I thought he was leaving us there, but the door stayed opened. Then he turned around and waved to us to get on the bus. He explained to the driver that my sister and I had boarded the wrong bus. After that explanation, we stayed on the extended-route bus without any additional fees. That was very nice of him.

Locked Out

I constantly followed Dianne's lead, that is why we got off the bus at the wrong stop. Dianne had a behavior method about her that allowed her to convince people to believe everything she said. In those early years of growing up I was just the naive (yes bad ass) little brother that accepted my big sister's lead regarding everything. Throughout our entire early childhood years, I got blamed for situations or terrible things that occurred. If Dianne dropped a mirror, drinking glass, or plate and if it broke, she would blame it on me. One time Dianne scratched a 45-vinyl record, "Big Chief," by Professor Long Hair. Dianne was so scared that my mom would find out, that she took the 45, handed it to me, and told me to go and throw it down in the drainage in front of the house. I can remember many days my mom inquiring what happened to that record, and while my mom was probing herself rationally and questioning us, Dianne would look at me with a mean face as in saying, if I snitched on her, that would be my last day on planet earth. The "shifting" blame to me for bad situations would occur up until my freshman year of high school. Let's just say I got punked around and beat up many times by my sister, but what is crazy, I loved the hell out of her, and if someone would put a hand on my sister, they would have to answer to me.

Hence, when I was around ten or eleven years old, while living on Law St. in our nice little yellow brick home with the pool in the back yard, my mom and stepdad, were taking an all-day trip one summer day. My mom made plans with our old neighbors back in The Village on Annette St. to take us in one day, so my mom instructed my sister and I to go and stay with some friend's back on Annette St. because of this appointment they had to attend. The friend's home back in The Village was only walking distance, about two miles, so that early summer morning we took off walking. We stayed there in The Village all morning and through noon time and later that evening until Dianne got bored and restless and decided we should head back home. Our old neighbors whom we were staying with did nothing to hold us back, so we took off to return home in defiance of my mom's order. I told my sister as we were walking home that I had a key to the back door so we could get in. When we arrived at our house, our parents were not there, so Dianne took the back-door key from me and walked around to the side of the home to open the back door while I stayed in front of the home. Before we all left home that early morning, my mom had attached the chain lock on the inside of the door; therefore, Dianne could not open the door all the way, but only about two inches because the chain lock prevented her from pushing the door all the way open. No problem. Dianne decided to go with plan-B to get into our house, and I listened to the "RINGLEADER," Dianne, regarding what plan-B attempt would require of us to get into the house. What my sister suggested was to try to get in through one of the windows, hoping one window was left unlocked. Therefore, Dianne seized a trashcan from the side of the house to use as a ladder and she placed it under the window in the front of our home and told me to climb up to see if the window was unlocked. Like a naïve little brother, I did what my big sister instructed me to do, but plan-B was unsuccessful because the window was locked. After I stepped down off the trashcan, Dianne walked toward the back of the house again because she still had the back-door key. She once again went to open the back door, her now plan-C attempt to get into the house.

I decided to sit down on the steps of the front porch and work through my boredom, so I grasped the water hose that was under the front window and turned on the water and just sat there splashing water against the trashcan, the house, and the window. Why? I have no idea, just something to do. All I knew was that I was having fun entertaining myself with the water hose, not knowing that lurking in the stars was a major event developing.

As I am still sitting, splashing water up against the trashcan, shockingly the front door to our home opens from the inside, and it scared the hell out of me. I looked up, and it was my sister, wow, plan-C did work. I asked, *"Dee, how ya got in da house? What cha do?"* As I walked into the house, she showed me how she got in. She literally pushed and pushed on the back door until the inside door trimming, where in the chain/lock was attached to, detached from the wall, and felled to the floor. Dianne asked me to help her reattach the wood trimming around the door to the wall, so I got a hammer and tried my best to hammer the door seal back in place. Case solved, right? Yes - now we are in the house. We have food to eat, TV to watch, and all the luxuries of a home with no parents. The good life!

A couple of hours later our parents finally arrived home and the trashcan we utilized trying to get into the front window was still under the front window and the screen was hanging half off the window. I am in the back den-room sitting in front of the television, so I did not see the anger on my mother's face as she enters the house. She proceeded first straight into my sister's room and started probing her as to why we were home and how did we get into the house and why was the trashcan under the front window of the home. Now I start to hear my mother's voice get louder and louder in Dianne's room as she was scolding her about not staying at the old neighbor/friend's house.

Then it went silent in Dianne's room, so I thought everything was ok. At that moment, my mom came out of Diane's room and started approaching me without saying a word and the next thing that happened, really happened, and I'll let you, the reader, use your imagination for this part of the story.

I kept telling my mom I did not do it, but she refused to believe me. Let me explain something for the sake of not embarrassing my mom. She was a good Mother. I probably would have responded the same way she did, had my own kids blatantly disrespected my instructions, broke into our home by busting through the back door, then trying to cover it up by hammering the door wood trimming back up and left the trashcan in front of the window out in front of the house with the screen for the window still hanging halfway off the window, what else was she supposed to do? Send the victim to time out? Sure!!!

Earlier in Dianne's room when I could not hear what was being discussed, Dianne told my mom that I was the mastermind of this entire incident. Yes, my sister lied to my mom. My sister said that I had suggested to her that we should go home because I had a key to the back door and that I placed the trashcan under the front window trying to get in and when that did not work, I pushed in the back door until the chain lock attached to the door trimming fell off. All the plans and actions were my idea according to Dianne and that is why my mom responded the way she did. The truth of the matter is that this was Dianne's plans A, B, C "and punishment" that I received that day. She eventually admitted the truth to my mom several days later. In the famous words of R & B artist, James Brown. There was going to be "THE BIG PAYBACK." Yes, the stars are now starting to line up against Dianne for a future occasion. Yes, Big Dee, this day would not go un-remembered. There are some cold January days ahead.

The Unexpected, Unplanned Pool Party

Swimming was my major interest every summer, and in the backyard of our home on Law Street, we had a wonderful four-foot-high, fifteen-foot-across, aboveground swimming pool. I was in fifth grade, and Dianne was in eighth grade; it was a Sunday afternoon in the late spring of 1969. I was watching TV and not swimming because of the dog-bite injury I had on back of my left leg. During that spring, I had worked hard, preparing the pool for hot, sunny days, and it was full of water and ready for action. If it were not for the injury, I would have, without a question, been swimming already. But, instead, on this quiet, calm Sunday afternoon, I was in the house, watching TV, and my mom was making over a lady's hair.

My mom was the best at washing, setting, and relaxing ladies' hair. Ladies would often come over to our home to get their hair made over, and that is how my mom earned some extra cash. Trust me, my mom was good at this; she should have opened her own business.

Surprisingly, the doorbell rang, and it was a boy from my sister's eighth-grade class at Epiphany. He said he was there for the pool party. I asked him what pool party, and he responded by giving me our address, the one he said Dianne had given to him.

I asked my mom about the pool party, but she didn't know anything about it either.

I invited the boy in anyway and showed him our pool. As we left the backyard and walked back to the front yard, just then, I saw my sister and several girls, her classmates, from Epiphany, walking up to our home. My sister and those girls walked into the front gate, laughing and giggling, already in bathing suits under their clothes. They all went straight along the side of the house to the backyard, took off their clothes, and jumped in the pool.

Just like that, there was a pool party!! And I had no idea.

I ran in the house and told my mom. She said nothing and continued working on that lady's hair.

Now I'm thinking very angrily to myself, *Hey, this is my pool.*

Because of the dog-bite injury on the back of my leg that I described back in chapter seven, I couldn't swim in the pool that I'd cleaned and prepared for the summer. But there they were, my sister's classmates, having a wonderful time in the pool that I cleaned, filled with water, treated with chlorine, repaired, and changed the filter in the pump.

What do I get in return? I get to watch spoiled Creole kids enjoy my pool! Not fair!!!!

Let's start keeping score.

Score
Dianne - 5 , Herman-0

I went back into the house and continued to watch TV. The doorbell rang again and again, like clockwork. Each time, there were several more of my sister's friends at the front door, ready for the unexpected pool party. I accompanied them to the backyard along the side of our home, watched them jump into MY pool, and I returned to watching TV. Once all the "undesirable" guests had arrived at the "unplanned" pool party, there were about thirty kids—those rotten Creole kids from Epiphany—in my four-foot-high, fifteen-foot-wide aboveground pool.

I knew there were too many people in the pool. My mom said nothing; she just let them swim and enjoy Dianne's "unplanned" pool party.

The kids started standing up on the sides of the pool in order to dive into the water. You should not do that with an aboveground pool. The first thing that could happen is you could fall backwards and injure yourself.

My mom came outside to the pool, looked around, said nothing, and went back in the house. I could not believe it. She was permitting my sister to have a pool party. Maybe my mom and Dianne planned this without my knowledge. If they did, that was wrong. If my sister did not plan to have a pool party and just invited a couple of friends over to swim, then that couple of friends turned out to be her entire eighth-grade class from Epiphany School.

My mom felt sorry for me as she observed my watching the kids having a good time in my pool, which I had not had a chance to enjoy. My mom asked could she look at the dog bite on my leg. So, she pulled back the bandage, examined the scar, and said it looked almost healed. She then gave me the liberty to jump in the pool too.

I was finally in my own pool, and we were all having a good time—unplanned pool party! Thanks, Dianne!!!

The kids kept climbing onto the sides of the pool and pushing off from there to jump in the water; that was causing the pool's walls to shake. First, the girls started doing this on one side of the pool. Then, several boys starting doing the same thing on the other side of the pool. As the kids kept doing this, the thick-rubber pool lining at the bottom of the pool slowly shifted from under the pool and started sticking out. The more the kids jumped up and down on top of the pool wall, the more the water pressure shifted the liner out from under the pool wall, causing the pool wall to sag and tilt. Crazy! Imagine that, really. One side of the pool wall was now up on top of the rubber that enclosed the water; the pool was now lopsided.

Everyone started getting out on the lower side of the pool. I ran in the house to tell my mom. She came out, looked at the situation, shook her head, and then politely asked everyone to leave. My sister was scared. The unplanned pool party was now over.

Everyone was standing there, just gazing at the elevated wall of the lopsided pool. Several boys thought it was funny, and one guy got the idea to stick some holes in the rubber with a safety pin he had in his clothes.

I screamed, *"No! Don't do dat!"* I knew that would cause an explosion, and I knew to repair the pool now, all I had to do was let the water out and then reposition the wall properly above the rubber lining.

As I am screaming, *"Stop, don't do that,"* these two stupid Creole boys pierced the rubber and then stood there watching and laughing as the water squirted out the little holes. Then suddenly and unexpectedly, the rubber right in front of them abruptly erupted with a powerful surge. Those laughing boys got knocked down by the gushing water, and it pushed them eight or ten feet back against the fence. All the girls started screaming hysterically and running.

I happened to be standing several feet away from the eruption and observed with sadness as the gushing water rushed down the side of the house to the front yard. The unofficial pool party was now officially over. Surprisingly, my mom did not get upset; I could not believe it. I was sad and miserable, and I wanted revenge on someone. That was my pool, and those ridiculous Creole kids destroyed it.

My mom, instead of getting upset, just said, *"We'll get it fixed."*

Wait! There was no "WE" in getting it fixed; it would only be up to me to fix it. Dianne sure was not going to fix the pool, nor was my stepdad.

To make a long story short, the pool was repaired, and you know who repaired it. Another score for Dianne.

Score
Dianne – 10 , Herman-0

Swimming at Pontchartrain Beach

Moving forward to my sister's early high school years and my middle school years, I would catch the city bus to Pontchartrain Beach Amusement Park, by myself, to go swimming during the summer.

As discussed earlier, I worked on Saturdays, so I had money that allowed me the freedom to travel throughout the city on the RTA, New Orleans's Regional Transit Authority, the bus system. The RTA enabled you to go any place in the city at a cost of only 10 cents. To travel on the bus back in the late sixties and early seventies was a luxury.

One Sunday afternoon, I had plenty of money to cover the $1.50 ticket to gain entrance into Pontchartrain Beach. That ticket was an "all-day, any-ride ticket" and swimming pool pass. I never favored the amusement rides or games at "the Beach," as we described Pontchartrain Beach in our social circle; swimming was my interest.

I did not have the courage to ride the Zephyr roller coaster. I was always too frightened to get on that giant ride, even as an older married adult. Call me a chicken, a coward, or whatever, NO ROLLER-COASTER RIDES FOR ME!!!!

I only rode that Zephyr roller coaster one time, and I was forced to get on it when I visited the Beach with a friend of mine and his older brother. I was about eleven years old. When the coaster started going up the giant ramp, that is when I went under the seat. I thought I was going to die as the Zephyr roller coaster rushed down the ramp. I never rode that roller coaster again.

So, on this hot Sunday afternoon, I went to the Beach by myself to go swimming. I knew early that day that my sister and some of her friends from Clark High School, would be there too, so, I looked out for them throughout the day. I never saw my sister and her friends, so I just hung out by myself and went over to the big pool to swim.

At the big pool, there was a high diving board about one hundred feet high—well, it seemed that high to me. But, realistically, it was about fifteen feet high. I had already learned how to swim in Miami and Poplarville at an early age, and diving out of trees into the creek in Poplarville was normal. On this Sunday afternoon, I was going up and down the big pool's diving-board ladder, jumping and diving into twelve feet of water.

The lifeguard attentively watched me when I first started, so I climbed up the ladder, stepped out onto the board, and dove in the pool of water, then swam up. After about two or three dives, he realized I knew what I was doing, so he was less tense about the situation.

Sidenote here: It would not surprise me to find out I was one of the first Black kids to swim in the big pool and dive off that high diving board, because every time I went to the Beach, there were never any other minorities that I can remember in the pools.

After several dives that day, I swam to the side of the pool as you normally do to get out, and when I looked up, there was my sister, standing outside the pool's fence, watching me with a very strange look of fear and worry on her face. I wondered what was going through her mind. Maybe she was reminiscing about her experience in Miami when she dove off the diving board, sunk to the bottom of the pool, and almost drowned.

I climbed out of the pool, walked over to where she was standing, and began talking through the fence. I remember she asked me, *"How deep da water is?"* I told her, and she asked, *"Yaw naw scur?"*

I said no and told her to stay there and watch as I went up and dove again. I wanted to show her how safe it was once someone knew how to swim. So, I went back up the ladder, dove in, swam to the edge of the pool, got out, and went back over to speak with her again.

After that dive, I think she felt better. I sincerely believe all her fears about swimming went away after seeing her skinny little brother dive off a fifteen-foot board into twelve feet of water and swim out of the pool safely.

The Dish-Towel Champion

NEVER, NEVER, NEVER should anyone interrupt my sister while she's washing dishes. There were no dishwashers back then, or if there were, we did not have one in 1973. Whenever I would annoy or pick a fight with my sister while she was washing dishes, she would retaliate with a wet dish towel, striking me with it. I would deliberately taunt her because I knew it would aggravate her, and I enjoyed dodging her attempted swings with the towel. To me, it was a competitive battle to see if she could actually hit me. Maybe two out of ten attempts would land on me, usually on my arms. So in the overall dish-towel-swinging challenge, I won and would joke with her about how terrible she was at swinging that dish towel.

Dianne's would shout with joy when landing any hit because the result for me would be immense stinging and pain that would leave a mark on my arms. She was a champion with that dish towel when those swings landed. The dish towel was her weapon of choice, and she often used it while washing dishes daily. I never hit my sister or fought back, ever, even when in intense pain. For me, I basically instigated the dish-towel battles as a game. I deserved many of those whacks from her weapon of choice.

But on a future date, that weapon of choice would align with the stars that were lining up against her.

In 1973, my sister, a senior in high school, is one of the most popular girls in her senior class. At night, the phone at our home rings all the time for her. Another way I would aggravate my sister is whenever the telephone would ring, if the call was for her, I would listen in on her conversations, on another phone in the other room. I would hold my hand over the mouthpiece so no room noises could be heard, and sometimes it would work. But when it did not work and she knew I was listening, she would physically beat me up.

But I deserved it.

I have concluded that I must have liked punishments from my sister because I constantly did many things that I knew aggravated her. I often called her offensive names and would embarrass her by taunting her in front of her friends. I am sure that anyone who has younger siblings understands all the things that they do. I did it all. I would get beat up for it, but for me that was okay, as long as Dianne, and no one else, was doing the beating.

Score

Dianne - 15 , Herman-0

To the Moon, Dianne, to the Moon

Our parents were away one school night, and my mom instructed Dianne to make sure I took a shower before falling asleep. I was in ninth grade at the time, and this was a week or two before my scarlet-fever incident.

On this rainy, cold January night, I fell into a deep sleep on the couch in the den in front of the TV because I was extremely tired due to my early morning school. Unexpectedly, I was awakened by someone beating me on my head and the middle of my back and yelling at me to get up and take a shower. I opened my eyes, and it's my sister. I sat up on the couch as she left the room, but I was so weary I could not get up. I lay back down and fell into a deep sleep once again on the couch.

Next thing I knew, I felt the weapon of choice, the wet dish towel, against my arm and back as Dianne is screaming, *"Get up; go take a shower befo Mama get home."*

Over the years, I had become accustomed to the dish-towel whackings; it was not as if I had not been whacked before. So, for a second time, I got up and sat on the couch for a short while.

Then I walked into the kitchen and asked her if she had the clean clothes out of the dryer, because I needed some clean underwear to put on after showering. Now, the washing machines and dryer were in the shed, which was in the backyard, outside past the pool. It was a very rainy, wet, cold, and windy January night.

Dianne answered me and said the dry clothes were still in the dryer out in the shed. So, I left the house, no shirt and no shoes, and I ran to the shed in the dark, through cold, wet, freezing nighttime weather and arrived at the clothes dryer. Once I opened its door, I discovered there were no clothes in the dryer, not a one. There I stood, puzzled and confused, wondering why there were no clothes in the dryer when Dianne told me there were.

I ran back into the house and said, *"Dee, you tol' me da clothes wa in the dryer; they ain't der. Wher dey at?"*

She started laughing and said, *"I don' know."*

So, I begged, *"Come on, tell me wher dey at?"*

She continued to laugh, as if we were playing a game, and started moving towards her room. She then turned around in this small hallway, right before her room, and she stretched her arms to both side walls, as if her body were a barricade in the hallway between me and her room.

So again I asked, *"Dee, please jus tell me wher dey at?"*

She responded, *"Da clothes are in my room, and ya can't go in der to get um. Stay out my room."*

I am standing there thinking to myself, *I am tired, sleepy, exhausted, frustrated, and aggravated. I just got beaten in the back and on my head while sleeping on the couch. Then she whacked me with her weapon of choice, several times. I have painful scorch marks on my arms. Then on top of that, she hoodwinked me into going outside in the wet and cold, —barefooted, no shirt—to get clothes out of the dryer that she knew were in her room. She deliberately deceived me for her personal entertainment and was probably raucously laughing at me while I was running to the shed outside in the wet, freezing, windy night, with no shoes and no shirt on.*

THE STARS HAVE ALIGNED! Goodbye dish towel...for good.

One of Jackie Gleason's favorite lines when he played Ralph Kramden in the classic TV sitcom *The Honeymooners* was "To the moon, Alice, to the moon."

Now, it is… *"To the moon, Dianne, to the moon!!!"*

As she stood there in that small hallway, using herself to block me from entering her room, I am literally begging her to give me some underwear.

As I approach her several times, she pushes me back, again, again, and again. This goes on for about five minutes as I am shouting and begging her to let me get some underwear out of her room. She stands there laughing and poking fun at me. I try once again, but this time, she uses her legs to kick me back.

So now I am done. What she considered just another traditional sibling challenge will now come to an end. My endurance and respect for my sister have left the room, and now my frustration has increased violently. I quickly make a fist with my right hand, rear back with fury, and punched her in the middle of her face. It was not premeditated; it was just a pure provoked emotional reaction.

To the moon she went, to aligned with the stars.

Dianne burst into a cry that was so loud, like a fire alarm, and, coincidentally, our parents were walking into the house through the front door at the "exact same time" I hit her. Dianne's loud scream caused my parents to think someone had broken into the house and was attacking us. They ran farther into the house hysterically, to find Dianne standing there crying while holding her face. Her little brother, who now is almost fifteen years old and no longer a little kid, but a high schooler like her, had never fought back until that night.

Honestly, I was expecting my mom would respond angrily, so I prepared for some type of punishment. I was thinking they would ship me off to the juvenile center, and that image scared the hell out of me, based on the horror stories I'd heard about the place. I went into my room while my mom helped Dianne; they went into her room to talk.

Dianne's the oldest and smartest, and her story is always believable. I hoped she would not make up a lie. As I stayed in my room and waited, I could only imagine what was about to happen to me. I just hoped I would not black out.

I was expecting my mom to enter my room vehemently irritated, but to my surprise, she entered somewhat calmly. I told my side of the entire story, and I showed her the wounds and bruises on my arms and back from the weapon of choice, the dish towel.

After a complete investigation of what happened, my mom realized that I finally could not take another physical beating or harassment from Dianne. My mom had allowed her to get away with beating me up and bossing me around for many years, but I was older now I knew when it is time to play and when to be serious.

My mom went back in the front of the house and spoke with Dianne. I could hear her telling Dianne to stop whacking me with the dish towel; I was not a little baby kid anymore. I was shocked; my mom backed me one hundred percent, but did not excuse me for punching Dianne in the face.

Then my mom came back to my room to give me my punishment for the face hitting.

Okay, I know! It's "house jail" for the weekend…right? NO!!

My punishment for hitting Dianne was that I had to wash dishes too. What kind of punishment is that for a fourteen-year-old boy? Boys do not wash dishes!! I cannot let my friends know about this because they would surely call me a sissy.

My mom explained that Dianne would do the dishes one week, and I would follow up the next week; we would alternate. So now I had an extra chore beside putting the trash out, cutting the grass, washing the car, and cleaning the pool. Now I must wash dishes too? Does Dianne cut grass or wash the cars? No! And what about the pool? Who should clean it? And on top of that, I had a job on Saturday mornings.

I need to really push this point. We were NOT violent kids. We never fought viciously physically; we just smacked on each other now and then, as typical siblings do, and nearly all the time, Dianne would get in two, three, or four more smacks than I did. But that night Dianne was more rude with me than she had been in the past, based on the bruises I showed my mom. We later found out why she was so emotionally annoyed.

Everyone reacts because of stress or pressure, and Dianne was under a tremendous amount of stress, about which none of us knew. It was her senior year, and Dianne was a smart, academically bright student. Honor roll student every year and NEVER missed a day of school. She was a member of the student government, a homecoming maid, and on the drill team while in high school.

That night, she had too much to do; she had to wash dishes, fold clothes, and study for two tests, plus try to make time to talk with her friends on the phone, which of course was her number one priority. So she was too stressed and tried to handle the situation the best way she could with her badass, little brother. Thus, she overreacted, trying to trick and trap me, and I overreacted too.

The hitting and punching me in the back and whacking me with the dish towel did not upset me, honestly. I was accustomed to that. What fueled my anger was the deliberate attempt to deceive me by sending me outside in the freezing cold, bare feet and all, knowing those clothes were not out there. I was maturing, I was no fool, and neither was she.

Unfortunately for Dianne, she had to take class pictures the next day.

As I stated early, the stars had been aligning against Dianne for a while, culminating with the events on this cold, wet night.

Score
Dianne - 15 , Herman- 5

My Sister's Academic Achievements

My sister attended Saint Mary's Academy, a Catholic school for girls. I was so glad she did. Our parents participated in every Saint Mary's school activity for the four years that Dianne was there. I always had to tag along to the school picnics, festivals, etc. I even started going to the Friday night dances as I got older. It seemed as if all the girls who went to St. Mary's would attend those dances. There were many pretty young ladies at St. Mary's. I became close friends with several of those young ladies and dated a couple of them too. I would not have had so many good times in my early high school years if it had not been for my sister attending Saint Mary's.

As I mentioned earlier, my sister was a very smart student—a straight-A student. At her graduation, I was immensely proud of her. She received acknowledgment trophies for just about every subject, and she received a big trophy for her "perfect four years' attendance" without missing a day. She was the only student to get that award. Wow. I remember carrying all those trophies; I was so proud to hold them as I was walking back to the car. It looked as if Dianne had more trophies that day than any other student graduating.

Sisters of the Holy Family building on Chef Menteur Highway, Eastern New Orleans.

Dianne was offered an academic scholarship to Oberlin College in Ohio. But my mom wanted to keep her close to the nest, so Dianne ended up attending the state's flagship school, Louisiana State University (LSU) in Baton Rouge, where she eventually received her bachelor's and master's degrees. Going to LSU was Dianne's time for integration; she had never attended an integrated school until LSU in the fall of 1973.

Score
Diane - 20 , Herman 5

LSU—1973 to 1978

The preceding chapter ended with me in tenth grade. I will now advance several years into the future to tell two unique stories involving my sister and me. Though there are many tales of our adventures and clashes, these next events are indicative of our sibling bond. I want to share experiences that reveal the relationship between my sister and me while we both attended LSU during the seventies. Geaux Tigers!!

I am sure that between 1950 and 1973 no more than 100-150 Black students attended LSU. Dianne and I were in that number. In 1971, the first Black athletes for the school competed in football and basketball.

During family gatherings, we joked about how I helped Dianne both socially and academically while we attended LSU together during her last two years there. Yes, I helped Dianne graduate from LSU. Even with all her high school achievements, she needed her little brother's assistance. Dianne needed me in a big way socially too.

My mom, in her clever futuristic foresight, understood why it was important for Dianne and me to attend a major university in the early seventies, especially in South Louisiana. Not speaking for Dianne, because she and I did not have a heart-to-heart conversation about her choice of colleges, but I wanted to attend a Historical Black College University (HBCU) because I was tired of the constant verbal racial harassment I had to endure throughout grammar school and my freshman year of high school. However, my mom knew for us to be competitive in the future, Dianne and I needed a quality education from a reputable university that would equip us with the skills to be competitive in an ever-changing business world, and help us assimilate with diverse cultures for future preparation in a progressive global economy. Thanks, Mom.

Dianne enrolled at LSU in the fall of 1973. It was very obvious that she was enjoying herself on campus because she never came home, except for holidays. Moving forward to the spring of 1974, Dianne invited me to visit LSU one weekend, so my best friend, Ricky, and I boarded a Greyhound bus and arrived on LSU's campus one late spring Friday afternoon. Dianne had asked a couple of brothers who lived in the LSU stadium dormitory to make room for me and my friend that weekend.

Yes, those windows you see on LSU's stadium were once dormitory rooms.

After arriving and settling in, we attended a dance that Friday night in the Catholic Student Center (CSC). There were only a handful of Black students attending LSU during this time, and it seemed that all of them were in the CSC that night. Ricky ended up spending the entire weekend in a coed dormitory with a female companion. We never saw him again, or the female student he "shacked up with," that entire weekend, until it was time to board the Greyhound bus back to New Orleans late Sunday afternoon.

That weekend changed my mind about attending any HBCU. My mom was right; I needed to attend LSU. I started telling all my high school friends that I was going to attend LSU after graduation.

In the summer of 1976, my sister helped me with registration; to ensure I would not flunk out my first semester, she selected simple classes for me. She also counseled me on where to live on campus, but left it to me to make the final decision. After hearing some great stories about all locations, I made my final choice—LSU stadium. That was my new home.

At the beginning of my freshman year in the fall of 1976, my sister was a junior and dating one of the best football players, whose position was running back. This guy was one of the premier players for LSU. He ended up being a high draft choice in the NFL. He played a couple of years in the NFL, moved to coaching in the NFL, and eventually coached for an NFL team that won the Super Bowl. At present, he is still an NFL coach. Dianne and this guy broke up at the end of her junior year, in the spring of 1977.

One day while in my dormitory room, the hall phone rang, and another person on our floor answered it. He came down the hall to my room, knocked on my door, and informed me I had a phone call. I went out into the hall to answer the phone, and it was my sister on the other end of the line. She was crying hysterically and trying to explain to me what just happened between her and this football player.

I was extremely angry after hearing what happened. No one, and I mean no one, is allowed to place a finger on my sister. No one. Dianne and he got into an argument. As she explained it, she turned away to leave the hostile conversation, but he grabbed her arm and wouldn't let go. She was twisting and trying to pull her arm from his firm grasp; then her watch fell off and broke. Forget the broken watch—his butt is mine now.

Remember, I am from New Orleans, an urban area. I have lived in the Upper and Lower Ninth Wards. So, my street and fighting skills were very well developed. Dianne was not there for all the fights I had during my middle and high school years. I had seen many violent incidents, some of which I have not included in this book. I couldn't care less that this football player is six three, 220 pounds, and can probably kick my butt in a New York second. I will stay cool and not chase him down or look for him. But I better not see his rural Louisiana butt, because, if I do, I will show him how urban New Orleans boys behave when you put your hands on their sisters.

Therefore, a couple of days later, not even thinking about what happened to Dianne, I am going to my LSU work-study job in the old Gym Armory building. This building was opened ever night for students to use for athletic activities. My job every evening from six to ten, was to sit at the front door and check and make sure only students with ID's could enter, to use the facilities to play basketball, volleyball, weight lift, dance, or roller skate. Down in the basement of this building other students worked in the equipment room. Students could borrow numerous sporting equipment, basketball, baseball bats, volleyballs...etc, with their ID's. As I am heading to work, I take this shortcut that is hardly used by students on campus. I am walking down the steps in this narrow passageway that is between the old Gym-Armory Building and the old Health and Physical Education Building (HPE). When I get to the bottom of the steps, I look to my right, and suddenly, out of nowhere, there he is, as if it was God's preordained plan for us to meet in a location that hardly anyone frequents. This location is one of the top-secret places on campus. It is a very narrow alleyway that hardly is ever used, even during daylight. I dare not tell you what couples can do in that location late into the dark night. Experience is the best teller.

I stopped when I saw him and stood there as he continued to walk towards me. He had a big bow and several arrows in his quiver; I assume he was on his way to return those objects to the HPE sports department, down in the basement of the old Gym Armory building. I was heading into the Old Gym Armory building too, to punch in for work.

Game on!

When he finally looked up and saw me, he stopped. I then bravely approached him and stopped directly in front of him, making eye-to-eye contact. In the toughest male tone voice I could muster, and without hesitation, I said in the most authentic ghetto-street dialect, *"Hey, bra, let me splain some-um to yaw, bra. I don know how y'all country boys handle y'all's beee-ness, but we city boys, we do dings diff-ernt. Don't put cha hands on my sista again."*

That is all I said; I did not let him respond. I turned around, and I walked away. I did not look back to see if he was about to attack me; I just boldly turned around and walked away.

Later that night, after I clocked out from my work-study job, and while walking to my stadium dormitory room, I realized what I had done. This gigantic, senior, athletic football player, first-team SEC, all-muscle, six-three, 220-pound jock with a bow and arrows in his hand could have trounced, crushed, and mangled my five-eight, 135-pound body, and jacked me up in "that location," and no one would have even seen or known. And then, experience could had told you how someone got their butt beat in that location. It would have been my word against his word. But he never even responded.

Very late that night when my sister knew I would be in my dormitory room after work, she called again. She asked what I had said to him, and I asked her why, what had she heard? Dianne said he visited her dormitory later that afternoon, after our confrontation, and summoned her to the lobby of her dormitory building to apologized, and he gave her a brand-new watch. Wow!

I then recounted the entire confrontation, and she kept asking what happened "after." I repeated several times that I had just walked away. My sister knew I was brave, but, before that, she had not known I was that brave enough to confront Mr. LSU Football, biggest guy on campus.

This guy was so esteemed on campus that one day while I was hanging out on the LSU Union steps and carousing with friends, a limousine pulled up, and it was Louisiana Governor Edwin Edwards. We were excited to see the Governor on campus, so we students all ran up to him to shake his hand. Mr. Football was walking out of the LSU Union doors while we were shaking the governor's hand, and when the governor saw Mr. Football, he broke away from us, and approached Mr. Football. Yes, you read that correctly. The Governor left us to walked over to meet Mr. Football, and they talked for several long minutes as we all watched.

Now that I look back on our confrontation, I had to protect my sister, and I am sure Mr. Football would agree I was the real big man on LSU campus that day

Score
Dianne - 20 , Herman- 15

My last Dish Towel Whack From My Sister

In another way, I was there for my sister, not for just one day, but for the entire semester. This story is not intended to embarrass my sister; she was academically smart. I see this in a comic sense, and if you knew my sister personally, especially throughout her professional career, you'd know this sequence that I am going to share is indicative of her behavior. She could manipulate a situation to her advantage instantly when it involved her and me.

My claim to fame is that without me—joking!—she would not have graduated from LSU. This is how I paid her back for all the people she "beat up" for me when we were growing up. I owed her this, and we laughed about this story all the time during family events.

At LSU in the spring of 1978, my sister and I had a geography class together. It was Geography 1001: Introduction to Geography, basically an elective.

This is how clever she was. She saved most of her easy elective courses for her last year of college so that she would not have to study so hard during her senior year. Now, that is smart!

She attended the first two or three classes of this freshman geography course, and after that, I received a one-on-one, private lecture from her. In this one-on-one conference, she pontificated about her position of not attending another class and gave me instructions regarding what I was to do.

I was instructed to attend geography class all semester and to give her all my lecture notes after each class. This was necessary because this class was, in the unbelievable words of my sister, *too early for her to wake up and attend.* It started at 9:00 a.m. three times a week. Are you kidding me?

So, without question, as the good little brother I was, I did not even argue with her. This was her last semester after five years, and it was only a freshman-level lecture course. All a person had to do to pass each test was read the lecture notes and the assigned textbook pages. I wish I could have found some knuckleheaded person who would have allowed me to copy their notes. It was not unusual to freely share lecture notes with someone who missed class for a legitimate reason.

But it was a challenge to find someone who would sacrifice their entire semester's attendance to benefit someone else. She found that knuckleheaded person—her brother. Metaphorically, she'd whacked me for the last time with the wet dish towel and made me do what she wanted.

The end results, Dianne passed the class, and I can claim two percent of her undergrad degree. Ha ha ha!!!!

Mr. Football One more time

After my sister graduated from LSU in 1978, she returned to our Eastern New Orleans home. Late one summer evening, I was returning home from being out and about all day, and I saw a brand-new Mercedes parked in front of our house. I knew Dianne started a new job with the Louisiana State Department of Social Services Division, so maybe she purchased her a new car. And if she did, I was excited to get into the house and ask her for the keys so that I could drive that fine-looking automobile, that thing was clean.

When I opened the front door, there in our living room was Mr. Football, one of his friends, and my sister. They turned and looked at me as I was standing there. I stood there for about three seconds, perplexed, saying to myself, *What the hell is he doing here?* Then, with the loudest outburst, they simultaneously started laughing hilariously out of control. I stood there another three / five seconds looking at them tyring to figure out what was so funny. I ignored their laughing because I had no idea what was so funny about me walking into my own home. Then I continued to walk to the back of the house, walking pass them while giving Mr. Football a mean gangster stare, while he is still laughing and looking at me. These knuckleheads are still laughing, and I have no idea what is so funny. I looked over toward my sister before I made it to the back of house, and she is literally rolling on the floor laughing. Ok, I am the butt of the joke.

I stayed in the back of the house until they left, controlling my emotions, still asking myself, what was so funny about me entering my home.

Come to find out later that night from my sister, they were describing to Mr. Football's friend the on-campus confrontation between me and Mr. Football, and that was when I opened the door. Yes, speaking of the devil. Just to make it clear, this city boy did not shake country boy's hand that night. And to make it even clearer, he would not have been allowed in our home that night had I been there when he arrived. Now I knew who the Mercedes belonged too. I should have asked him for the keys. Now that would have been funny.

Wow!!! Can you believe that? Two little Negro/Black kids, a brother and a sister—who grew up in the Ninth Ward, lived in the Desire Housing Project during the early sixties, in the Lower Ninth Ward on Alabo Street, and on Annette Street in the Seventh Ward—attending LSU in the early to mid-seventies, and the sister graduated with both a bachelor's and a master's degree from LSU!!

YOU GEAUX, GIRL!!!
Final Score
Dianne-100 , Herman-15

Dianne
7/16/1955...to...10/4/2019

My sister died after a hard battle with cancer.
She is deeply missed by her mother, two sons, ex-husband,
nieces, nephews, friends, sister-in-law, and, of course, me.

Author's Background

Born and raised in New Orleans, Louisiana, I lived in the Upper and Lower Ninth Wards most of my life. I also lived in the Seventh and Fifteenth Wards for a brief period. Growing up in the Desire Community of the Ninth Ward during the sixties, and being a person of a lighter skin complexion, sometimes presented its challenges. Most of those challenges were literally trying to prove to kids in our community, especially when we lived in the Desire Housing Projects, that I was Negro. The racial designations Black and African American were not politically correct terms during the early sixties. I hated and continually rejected being called *"White boy"* and was disturbed every time someone called me that. I hated it to the point that I would get into physical brawls as a small child just because someone called me "White boy."

One thing I knew, and I knew for sure—I was not White, and I did not want to be characterized as a White person.

I attended several different Catholic grammar schools. For kindergarten through second grade, I attended Saint Philip the Apostle, on Clouet Street in the Desire Community of the Ninth Ward. For third grade through the first half of fifth grade, I attended Epiphany Catholic School in the Seventh Ward. I finished the second half of fifth grade back at Saint Philip the Apostle. I then, in the fall of '69, attended Our Lady Star of the Sea, on Saint Roch Street in the Eighth Ward, for sixth, seventh, and half of eighth grades. I was one of the first six Black students to attend Our Lady of the Sea. Then I attended my first public school for the first half of eighth grade—Colton Junior High on Saint Claude Avenue in the Eighth Ward. I finished the second half of eighth grade back at Our Lady Star of the Sea, where I was one of the first three Black students to graduate from that school.

I attended three different high schools. My freshman year, 1972-1973, I attended Redemptorist Catholic High School in the Irish Channel. That school had over four hundred students. I was one of the first twelve Black students to attend Redemptorist. Because of the ongoing racial harassment by students at Redemptorist, I transferred to Alcee Fortier High School my sophomore year, 1973–1974.

Eleanor McMain Magnet, a new high school, was founded in the fall of '74, so I enrolled there for my junior and senior years before graduating in 1976.

Post high school, I attended Louisiana State University (LSU) in Baton Rouge for three uninterrupted years, 1976 to 1979, and my major was political science. My sister was already attending LSU; therefore, she and I were two of the first 100 -150 Black students to attend LSU.

I attended two summer-college sessions—one at the University of New Orleans (UNO), the summer of 1978, and the other at Southern University at New Orleans (SUNO), the summer of 1979. I changed majors from political science to elementary education and then transferred from LSU to UNO the fall of 1979, remaining there until 1981 without completing my degree.

Eventually, thirteen years later, I finished my college education through Concordia University Wisconsin's, extension/center in Metairie, Louisiana, while working full time, married, with two kids, and one daughter before marriage. I received a Bachelor of Arts degree in Business Management and Communications in 1994.